50일 영어낭독으로 원어민

ENGLISH for EVERYDAY ACTIVITIES

A Picture Process Dictionary

Lawrence J. Zwier

Activity Book

Contents

Section 1 Starting the Day

Section 2 Getting Around

Section 3 At Home in the Evening

Section 4 Managing a Household

Section 5 Keeping in Touch

Section 6 Having Fun with Friends

Section

1

Starting the Day

Scan for Audio

DAY 1 First Thing in the Morning

1. Filling in 그림 아래의 빈칸에 올바른 단어 혹은 구를 〈보기〉에서 찾아서 쓰시오. 〈보기〉의 단어 혹은 구는 한 번만 사용하시오.

brushing hair　drying off　ringing　shaving　waking up　washing

1. ______________________

2. ______________________

3. ______________________

4. ______________________

5. ______________________

6. ______________________

2. Sorting 각 문항마다, 먼저 일어나는 사건 옆에 숫자 "1", 다음에 일어나는 사건 옆에는 "2"를 쓰시오.

a. _____ getting out of bed　　_____ waking up
b. _____ taking a shower　　_____ drying yourself off
c. _____ flushing the toilet　　_____ using the toilet
d. _____ making breakfast　　_____ eating breakfast
e. _____ going into the bathroom　　_____ using the toilet

3. Listening 01 다음을 듣고, 문장을 완성할 수 있는 가장 올바른 답을 고르시오.

1. The man is ________.	ringing	waking up	leaving his apartment
2. The woman is ________.	taking a shower	eating	brushing her hair
3. The man is ________.	flushing the toilet	shaving	washing
4. The woman is ________.	waking up	making breakfast	eating breakfast

DAY 2

Brushing Your Teeth / Flossing

1. Filling in 그림 아래의 빈칸에 올바른 단어 혹은 구를 〈보기〉에서 찾아서 쓰시오. 〈보기〉의 단어 혹은 구는 한 번만 사용하시오.

back and forth **running** **squeezing** **rinsing** **spitting** **up and down**

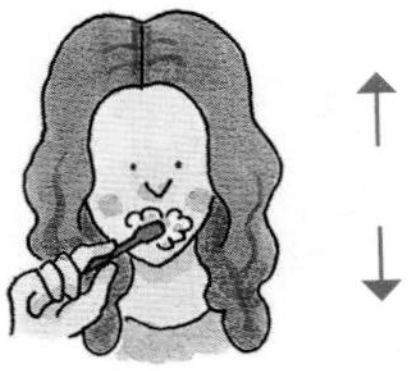

1. She's moving the toothbrush ________________.

2. She's ________________ some water over her toothbrush.

3. She's ________________ off her toothbrush.

4. She's ________________ water into the sink.

5. She's swishing water ________________ in her mouth.

6. She's ________________ toothpaste onto her toothbrush.

2. Matching 가장 올바른 설명을 B열에서 찾아서 A열 옆에 쓰시오.

	A	B
____	1. mouth	a. more than one tooth
____	2. toothpaste	b. it goes on a toothbrush
____	3. floss	c. it comes in long pieces
____	4. teeth	d. you rinse it off with water
____	5. toothbrush	e. your teeth are inside this

3. Listening 02 다음을 듣고, 문장을 완성할 수 있는 가장 올바른 답을 고르시오.

1. He's putting something ______.	between his teeth	into the sink	over his toothbrush
2. She's putting something ______.	on her toothbrush	in a rack	into her mouth
3. Something is coming out of ______.	a faucet	his mouth	a tube
4. Something is coming out of ______.	a rack	a faucet	a tube

Taking a Shower

DAY 3

1. Filling in 그림 아래의 빈칸에 올바른 단어 혹은 구를 〈보기〉에서 찾아서 쓰시오. 〈보기〉의 단어 혹은 구는 각 문항당 한 번만 사용하여, 2–5번 문항에는 두개의 나뉘어진 빈칸에 올바르게 넣어 완성하시오.

drying off | **stepping out** | **turning on** | **pulling shut** | **turning off** | **wrapping**

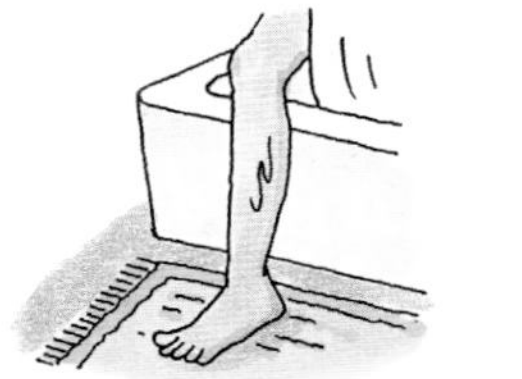

1. He is ______________ of the shower.

2. He is ______________ himself ______________.

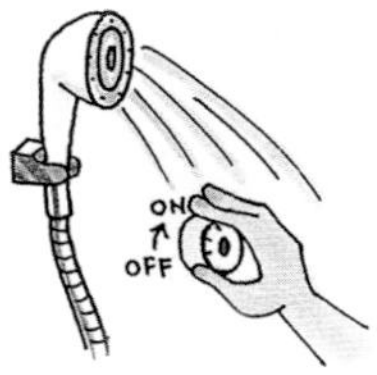

3. He is ______________ the water ______________.

4. He is ______________ the water ______________.

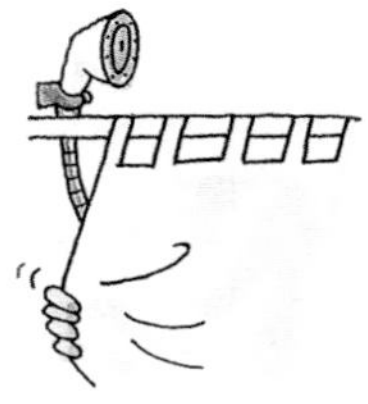

5. He is ______________ the curtain ______________.

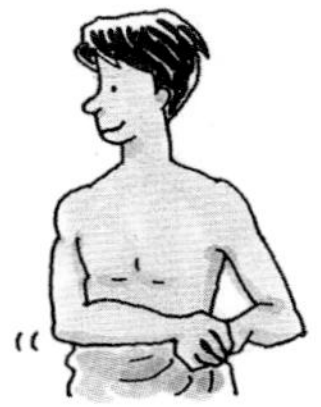

6. He is ______________ a towel around himself.

2. Matching 가장 올바른 설명을 B열에서 찾아서 A열 옆에 쓰시오.

A	B
____ 1. rack	a. it takes away bad smells
____ 2. bathmat	b. a towel can be put on this
____ 3. shower head	c. you turn this
____ 4. deodorant	d. water comes out of this
____ 5. knob	e. this is on the floor, near the shower

3. Listening (03) 다음을 듣고, 문장을 완성할 수 있는 가장 올바른 답을 고르시오.

1. The man is using ______.	soap	shampoo	a shower curtain
2. The woman is using ______.	a towel	a bathmat	some water
3. The man is using ______.	a blow dryer	a towel	a shower head
4. The woman is using ______.	soap	shampoo	deodorant

DAY 4

Getting Dressed: A Man

1. **Filling in** 그림 아래의 빈칸에 올바른 단어 혹은 구를 〈보기〉에서 찾아서 쓰시오. 〈보기〉의 단어 혹은 구는 한 번만 사용하시오.

buckling	pulling	tucking	buttoning	straightening	zipping up

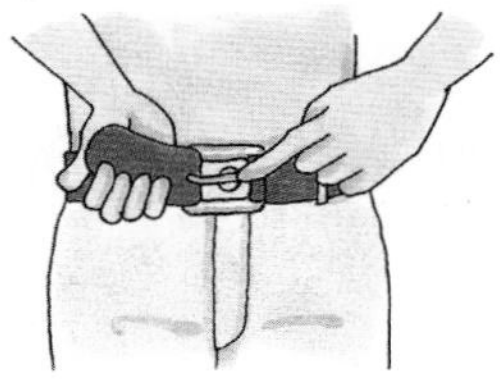

1. He is ______________ his belt.

2. He is ______________ his shirt.

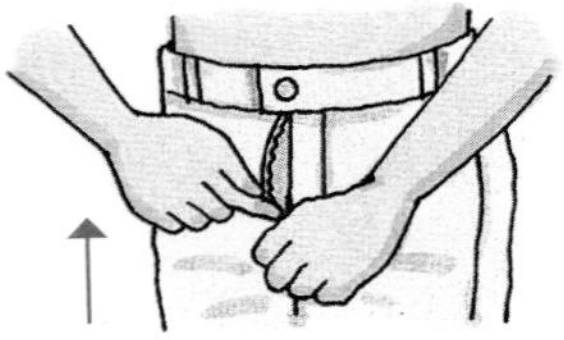

3. He is ______________ his fly.

4. He is ______________ his shirt into his pants.

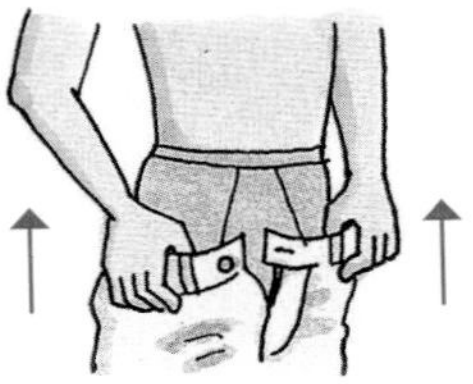

5. He is ______________ his pants up.

6. He is ______________ his collar.

2. **Sorting** 빈칸에 *some* 혹은 *a*와 함께 사용하는 단어를 〈보기〉에서 찾아 쓰시오.

glasses
jacket
pants
shirt
shoes
socks
underwear

	some	*a*
1.	______________	______________
2.	______________	______________
3.	______________	______________
4.	______________	______________
5.	______________	______________

3. **Listening** 04 다음을 듣고, 올바른 번호를 그림 옆에 쓰시오.

____ a. 

____ b. 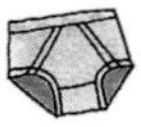

____ c. 

____ d. 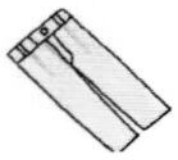

____ e. 

____ f. 

____ g. 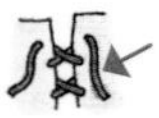

____ h. 

____ i. 

Getting Dressed: A Woman

1. Filling in 그림 아래의 빈칸에 올바른 단어 혹은 구를 〈보기〉에서 찾아서 쓰시오. 〈보기〉의 단어 혹은 구는 한 번만 사용하시오.

inside	outside	wearing	going	putting on	wrapping

1. She is ________________ a shirt.

2. She is ________________ the house.

3. He is ________________ the house.

4. She is ________________ a suit.

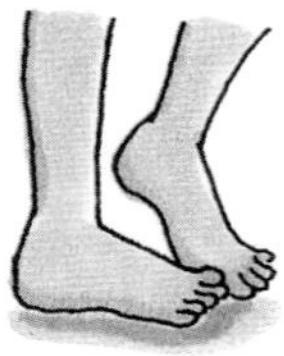

5. She is ________________ barefoot.

6. She is ________________ a scarf around her neck.

2. Matching 가장 올바른 설명을 B열에서 찾아서 A열 옆에 쓰시오.

	A	B
____	1. light clothes	a. a fabric that comes from sheep
____	2. heavy clothes	b. wearing these keeps you cool
____	3. wool	c. a fabric that comes from a plant
____	4. cotton	d. T-shirts, shorts, jeans, etc.
____	5. casual clothes	e. wearing these keeps you warm

3. Listening 05 다음을 듣고, 올바른 번호를 그림 옆에 쓰시오.

____ a. 

____ b. 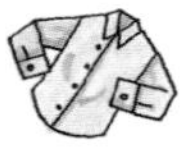

____ c. 

____ d. 

____ e. 

____ f. 

DAY 6

Making a Bed

1. Filling in 그림 아래의 빈칸에 올바른 단어 혹은 구를 〈보기〉에서 찾아서 쓰시오. 〈보기〉의 단어 혹은 구는 한 번만 사용하시오.

fluffing up   slipping   smoothing out   pulling   spreading   tucking

1. He is ________________ the pillow.

2. He is ________________ a sheet over the bed.

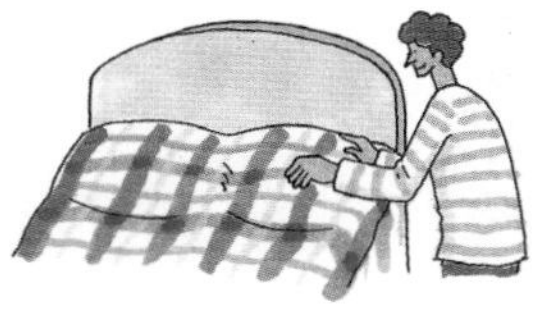

3. He is ________________ the bedspread.

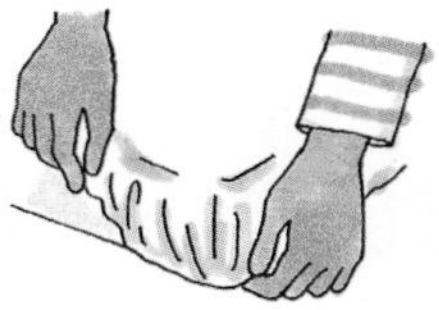

4. He is ________________ a fitted sheet over the mattress.

5. He is ________________ a sheet under the mattress.

6. He is ________________ a sheet tight.

2. Sorting 먼저 일어나는 사건 순으로 1부터 6까지 순서를 나열하시오.

____ a. laying pillows at the head of the bed
____ b. putting a bottom sheet on the bed
____ c. spreading a bedspread over the bed
____ d. putting a top sheet on the bed
____ e. spreading a blanket over the bed
____ f. smoothing out a bedspread

3. Listening 06 다음을 듣고, 언급된 단어 혹은 구를 고르시오.

1. bedspread	head of the bed	mattress
2. flat sheet	pillowcase	lay
3. tuck	fluff up	foot of the bed
4. flat	fitted	slip

Making Coffee / Making Tea

1. Filling in 그림 아래의 빈칸에 올바른 단어 혹은 구를 〈보기〉에서 찾아서 쓰시오. 〈보기〉의 단어 혹은 구는 한 번만 사용하시오.

dripping **pouring** **straining** **heating** **scooping** **turning**

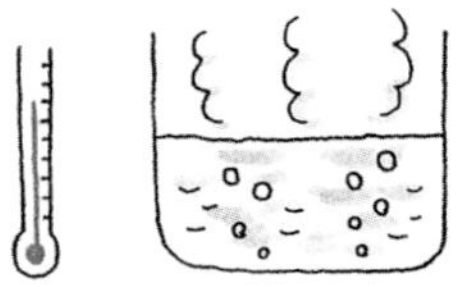

1. The water is _______________ up.

2. He is _______________ water into the teapot.

3. Water is _______________ through the ground coffee.

4. She is _______________ ground coffee into the filter.

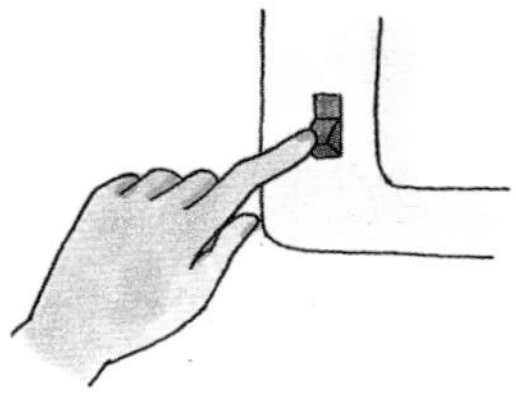

5. She is _______________ the coffee maker on.

6. He is _______________ the tea.

2. Matching 가장 올바른 설명을 B열에서 찾아서 A열 옆에 쓰시오.

A	B
____ 1. scoop	a. liquids pass through this; it has very small holes
____ 2. filter	b. liquids pass through this; it has larger holes
____ 3. strainer	c. this goes under a teacup
____ 4. teakettle	d. this holds hot water and tea leaves
____ 5. saucer	e. this is used to pick up ground coffee

3. Listening 07 다음을 듣고, 언급된 단어 혹은 구를 고르시오.

1. teapot	teacup	coffeepot
2. pressing	boiling	pouring
3. tea leaves	heating	adding
4. switch	drips	filter
5. pot	on	hot

DAY 8

Preparing Breakfast

1. Filling in 그림 아래의 빈칸에 올바른 단어 혹은 구를 〈보기〉에서 찾아서 쓰시오. 〈보기〉의 단어 혹은 구는 한 번만 사용하시오.

peeling cracking spreading popping slicing sprinkling

1. The toast is ________________ up.

2. He is ________________ sugar on his cereal.

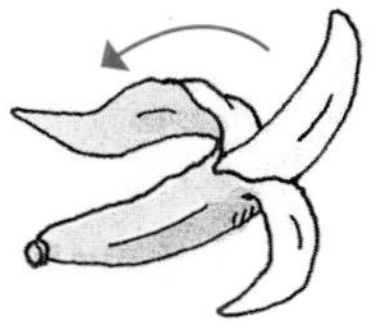

3. She is ________________ the banana.

4. She is ________________ an egg.

5. She is ________________ jam on her toast.

6. He is ________________ the banana.

2. Labeling 올바른 단어 혹은 구를 〈보기〉에서 찾아서 쓰시오.

bowl
butter
cereal box
jam
knife
a slice of bread

1. ________________
2. ________________
3. ________________
4. ________________
5. ________________
6. ________________

3. Listening 08 다음을 듣고, 문장을 완성할 수 있는 가장 올바른 답을 고르시오.

1. bowl	box	toaster
2. a knife	some milk	a bowl
3. banana	butter	bread
4. pop the toast up	lower the bread	raise the bread
5. sugar	milk	cereal

DAY 9

Eating Breakfast

1. **Filling in** 그림 아래의 빈칸에 올바른 단어 혹은 구를 〈보기〉에서 찾아서 쓰시오. 〈보기〉의 단어 혹은 구는 한 번만 사용하시오.

dipping **leaving** **sitting** **drinking** **reading** **wiping**

1. She is ________________ the news.

2. He is ________________ his toast into the egg yolk.

3. She is ________________ some coffee.

4. They are ________________ down at the table.

5. She is ________________ her lips with a napkin.

6. She is ________________ the table.

2. **Labeling** 올바른 단어 혹은 구를 〈보기〉에서 찾아서 쓰시오.

bacon
bowl
egg
knife
spoon
toast
fork

1. ________________
2. ________________
3. ________________
4. ________________
5. ________________
6. ________________
7. ________________

3. **Listening** 09 다음을 듣고, 질문에 가장 알맞는 답변을 고르시오.

1. toast	cereal	tea
2. the news	cereal	the table
3. a knife	a napkin	toast
4. breakfast	an egg	coffee
5. the table	a spoon	breakfast

DAY 10

Leaving the House

1. Filling in 그림 아래의 빈칸에 올바른 단어 혹은 구를 〈보기〉에서 찾아서 쓰시오. 〈보기〉의 단어 혹은 구는 한 번만 사용하시오.

opening putting shutting picking up putting on zipping up

1. He is ______________ his shoes.

2. He is ______________ the door.

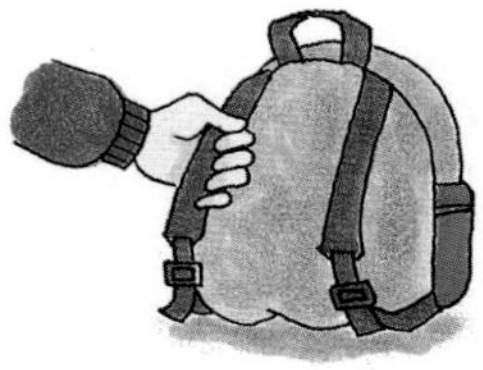

3. He is ______________ his backpack.

4. He is ______________ his key in his pocket.

5. He is ______________ the door.

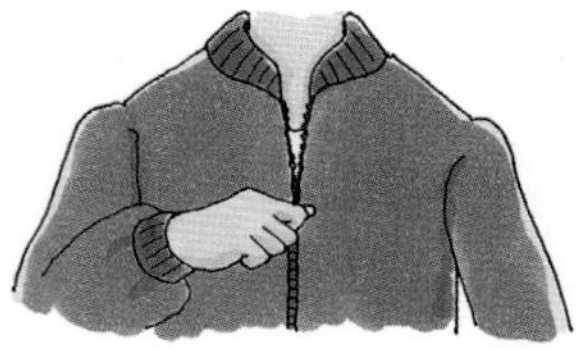

6. He is ______________ his jacket.

2. Matching 가장 올바른 설명을 B열에서 찾아서 A열 옆에 쓰시오.

A	B
____ 1. outside	a. a piece of clothing that can be worn over a shirt
____ 2. "See you later!"	b. not in the house
____ 3. backpack	c. a large bag, in which you can carry books and other things
____ 4. wallet	d. a thing in which you can keep money
____ 5. jacket	e. one way to say goodbye

3. Listening (10) 다음을 듣고, 질문에 가장 알맞는 답변을 고르시오.

1. shoes	a jacket	a backpack
2. shoes	a jacket	a backpack
3. outside	in the house	in a pocket
4. a shoe	a pocket	a wallet
5. opening a door	shutting a door	saying goodbye

Memo

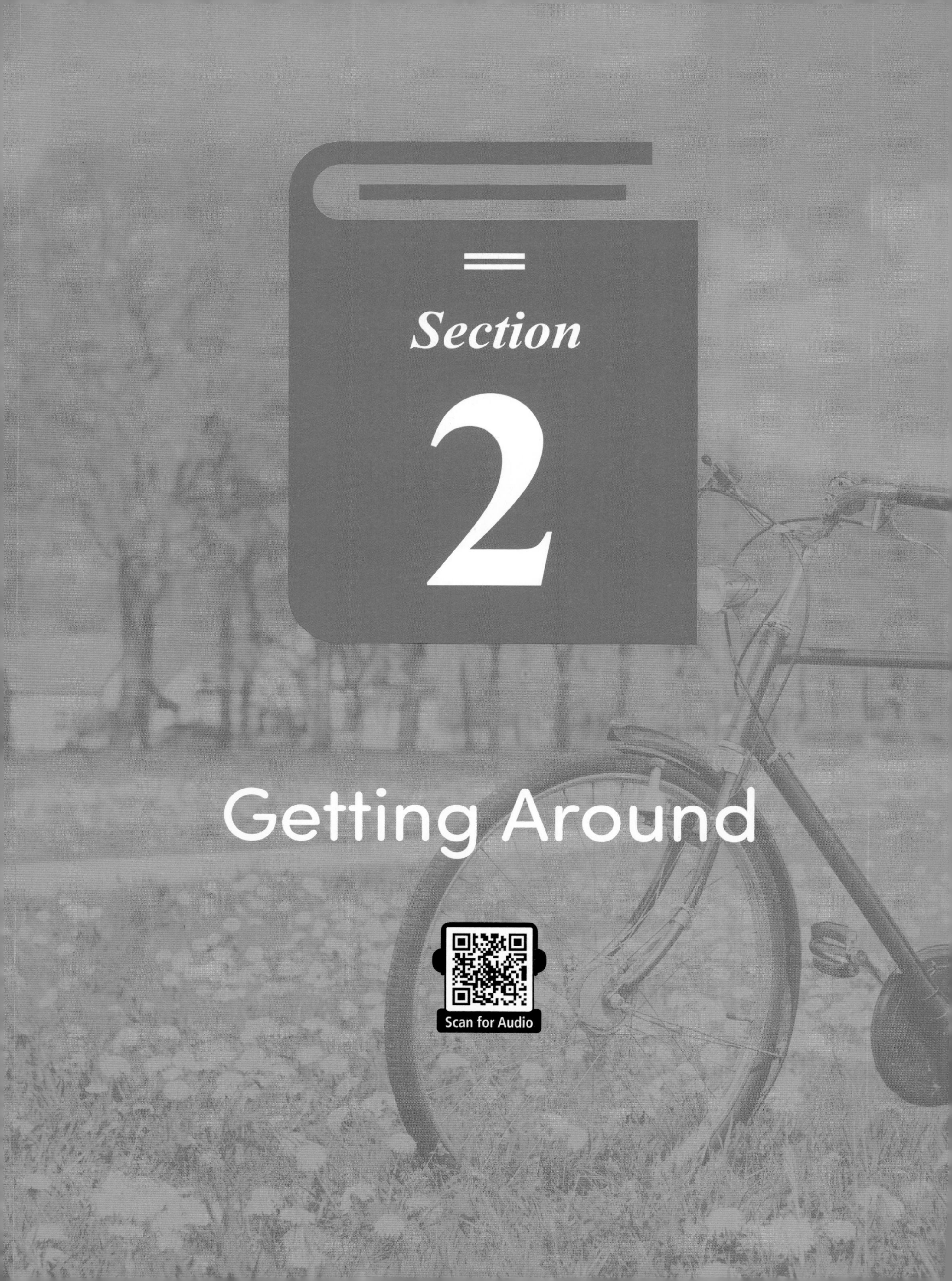

Section 2

Getting Around

Scan for Audio

DAY
11
Taking a Bus

1. Filling in 그림 아래의 빈칸에 올바른 단어 혹은 구를 〈보기〉에서 찾아서 쓰시오. 〈보기〉의 단어 혹은 구는 한 번만 사용하시오.

due	paying	waiting	full	pressing	walking

1. She is ________________ a button.

2. A Number 78 bus is ________________ at 8:30.

3. All the seats are ________________.

4. Someone is ________________ a fare.

5. She is ________________ to the bus stop.

6. She is ________________ at the bus stop.

2. Matching 가장 올바른 설명을 B열에서 찾아서 A열 옆에 쓰시오.

A	B
____ 1. full	a. having no empty places
____ 2. on time	b. a card or a piece of paper that lets you go somewhere
____ 3. fare	c. an open space between the seats of a bus
____ 4. pass	d. the money you must pay to ride a bus
____ 5. aisle	e. not late and not early

3. Listening (11) 다음을 듣고, 문장을 완성할 수 있는 가장 올바른 답을 고르시오.

1. The man is ______.	ringing a signal	getting on a bus	checking a schedule
2. The woman is ______.	showing a pass	paying a bus driver	opening a door
3. The man is ______.	sitting down	getting off the bus	standing
4. The woman is ______.	getting on a bus	getting off a bus	waiting for a bus

DAY 12

Starting a Car

1. **Filling in** 그림 아래의 빈칸에 올바른 단어 혹은 구를 〈보기〉에서 찾아서 쓰시오. 〈보기〉의 단어 혹은 구는 한 번만 사용하시오.

adjusting	buckling	shifting	backing	looking	pressing

1. She is ________________ the ignition.

2. She is ________________ over her shoulder.

3. She is ________________ out of the parking space.

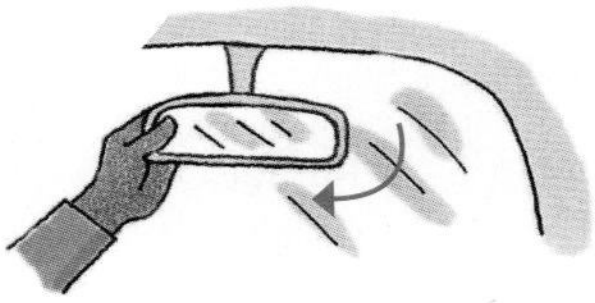

4. She is ________________ the rear-view mirror.

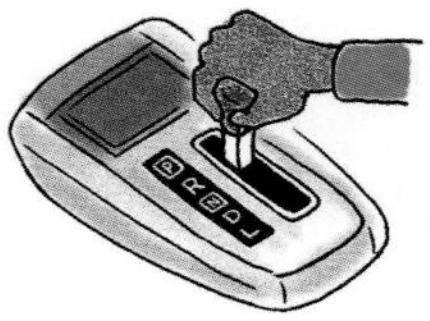

5. She is ________________ the gear into reverse.

6. She is ________________ her seat belt.

2. **Matching** 가장 올바른 설명을 B열에서 찾아서 A열 옆에 쓰시오.

A	B
____ 1. shoulder	a. the driver of a car sits here
____ 2. ignition	b. people who are not driving sit here
____ 3. accelerator	c. a part of a person's body
____ 4. driver's seat	d. a pedal that controls the speed of a car
____ 5. passenger seat	e. a mechanism that starts a car

3. **Listening** (12) 다음을 듣고, 각 문항의 상황과 가장 어울리는 것 옆에 번호를 쓰시오.

_____ a. The car has started.
_____ b. She's sitting in the driver's seat.
_____ c. He's backing out of a place.
_____ d. She's not the driver.
_____ e. He'll adjust the seat.

Driving Along

1. **Filling in** 그림 아래의 빈칸에 올바른 단어 혹은 구를 〈보기〉에서 찾아서 쓰시오. 〈보기〉의 단어 혹은 구는 한 번만 사용하시오.

changing lanes getting off turning left getting on going straight turning right

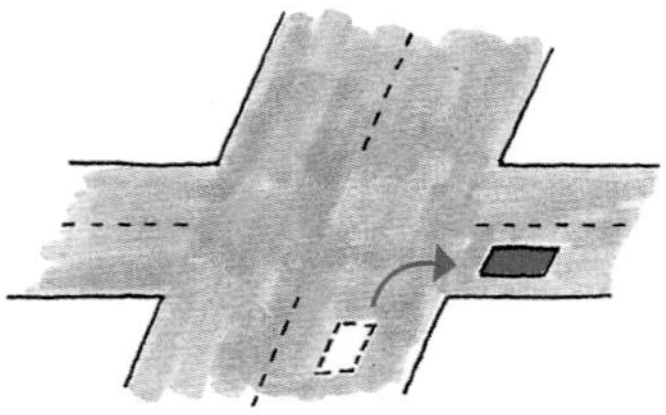

1. The car is ________________.

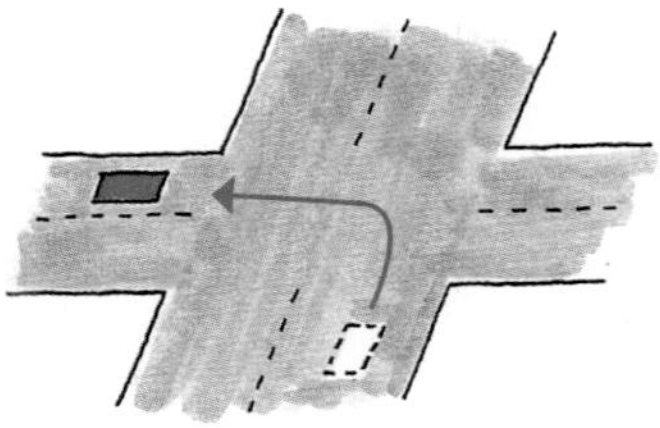

2. The car is ________________.

3. The car is ________________ a freeway.

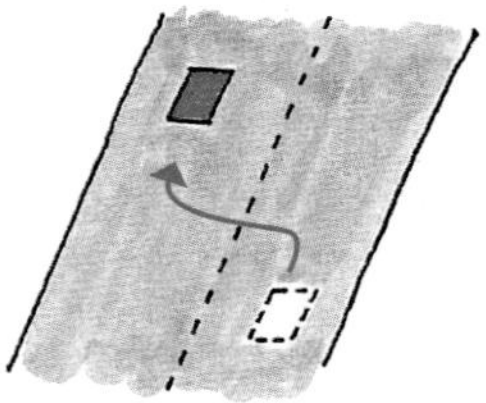

4. The car is ________________.

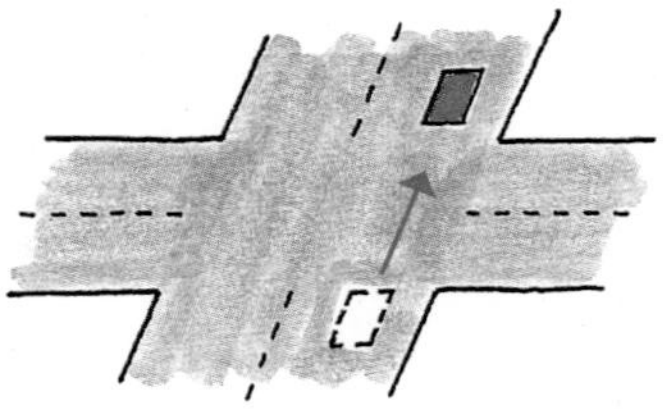

5. The car is ________________.

6. The car is ________________ a freeway.

2. **Matching** 가장 올바른 설명을 B열에서 찾아서 A열 옆에 쓰시오.

	A	B
____	1. intersection	a. you can pull up to this and get gas out of it
____	2. pump	b. you can pull into this to buy gas
____	3. speeding ticket	c. you should not go faster than this
____	4. speed limit	d. the police might give you this
____	5. gas station	e. a place where two roads meet

3. **Listening** 13 다음을 듣고, 각 문항의 상황과 가장 어울리는 것 옆에 번호를 쓰시오.

____ a. She's getting a ticket.
____ b. She's telling the attendant how much gas she wants.
____ c. She's paying for her gas.
____ d. She's saying what kind of gas she wants.
____ e. She's yielding right of way.

DAY 14 Taking a Train

1. Filling in 그림 아래의 빈칸에 올바른 단어 혹은 구를 〈보기〉에서 찾아서 쓰시오. 〈보기〉의 단어 혹은 구는 한 번만 사용하시오.

buying	getting on	standing	getting off	scanning	waiting

1. He is __________________ a train.

2. He is __________________ his ticket from a machine.

3. He is __________________ in a crowded train.

4. He is __________________ a train.

5. He is __________________ his ticket on the card reader.

6. He is __________________ for a train.

2. Matching 가장 올바른 설명을 B열에서 찾아서 A열 옆에 쓰시오.

A

____ 1. platform
____ 2. turnstile
____ 3. gate
____ 4. ticket window
____ 5. track

B

a. a gate that lets one person at a time to go through
b. the part of a train station that opens to let people through
c. a window through which tickets are sold
d. a flat place to stand near a track
e. a train rolls on this

3. Listening (14) 다음을 듣고, 문장을 완성할 수 있는 가장 올바른 답을 고르시오.

1. They are _______.	signs	crowded	passengers
2. He is at the _______.	platform	track	gate
3. She is looking at a _______.	sign	train	ticket
4. The station was _______.	crowded	announced	followed
5. Her train has just _______.	arrived	inserted	announced

DAY 15

Taking a Taxi

1. **Filling in** 그림 아래의 빈칸에 올바른 단어 혹은 구를 〈보기〉에서 찾아서 쓰시오. 〈보기〉의 단어 혹은 구는 한 번만 사용하시오.

checking giving paying getting into hailing starting

1. She is ________________ the driver directions.

2. She is ________________ the meter.

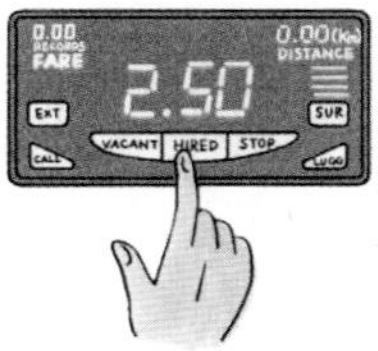

3. He is ________________ the meter.

4. She is ________________ the driver.

5. She is ________________ a taxi.

6. She is ________________ a taxi.

2. **Matching** 가장 올바른 설명을 B열에서 찾아서 A열 옆에 쓰시오.

	A	B
____	1. meter	a. instructions that tell someone how to get to a place
____	2. tip	b. the money you have to pay for your taxi ride
____	3. driver	c. extra money that's given to someone to thank them for giving you service
____	4. fare	d. a machine that tells how much you have to pay for a ride
____	5. directions	e. the person who gives you a ride

3. **Listening** (15) 다음을 듣고, 각 문항의 상황과 가장 어울리는 것 옆에 번호를 쓰시오.

_____ a. Someone is hailing a taxi.
_____ b. Someone is giving a tip.
_____ c. Someone is giving directions.
_____ d. Someone is saying where to stop.
_____ e. Someone is saying where she wants to go.

DAY 16

Walking Somewhere

1. Filling in 그림 아래의 빈칸에 올바른 단어를 〈보기〉에서 찾아서 쓰시오. 〈보기〉의 단어는 한 번만 사용하시오.

stepping **crossing** **taking** **running** **stopping** **tripping**

1. He is __________ a street.

2. He is __________ over dirt and puddles.

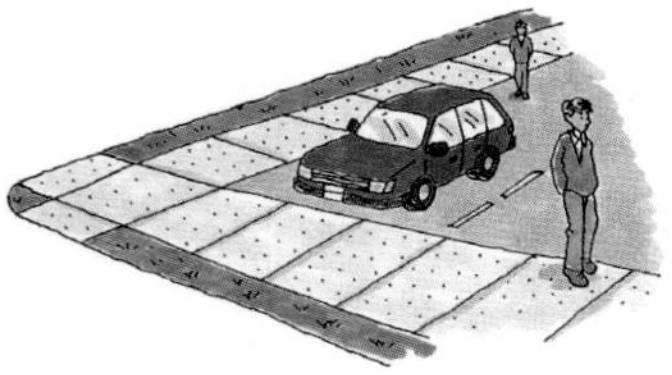

3. He is __________ a shortcut.

4. He is __________.

5. He is __________ on a crack in the sidewalk.

6. He is __________ at the curb.

2. Matching 가장 올바른 설명을 B열에서 찾아서 A열 옆에 쓰시오.

A	B
____ 1. pedestrian	a. someone who is walking
____ 2. shortcut	b. this goes above a road, and people can walk on it
____ 3. crosswalk	c. a place on the street where people should cross
____ 4. overpass	d. a way that is shorter than the usual way
____ 5. traffic	e. the cars or buses on a street

3. Listening (16) 다음을 듣고, 언급된 단어 혹은 구를 고르시오.

1. stopped	tripped	stepped
2. late	wait	street
3. pass	traffic	crack
4. sidewalk	across	crosswalk
5. trip	step	busy

Riding a Bicycle

DAY 17

1. **Filling in** 그림 아래의 빈칸에 올바른 단어 혹은 구를 〈보기〉에서 찾아서 쓰시오. 〈보기〉의 단어 혹은 구는 한 번만 사용하시오.

holding	pedaling	squeezing	locking	shifting	swinging

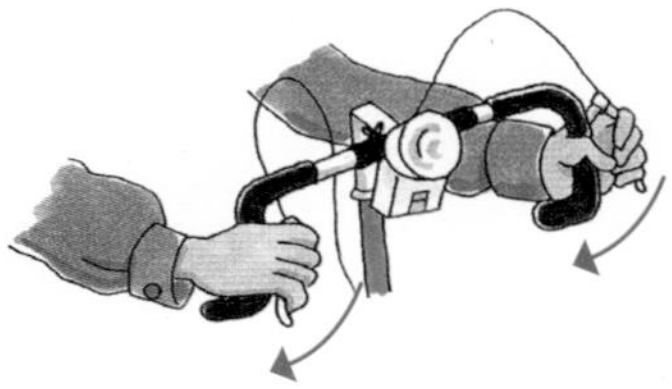

1. He is ________________ the brakes.

2. He is ________________, so the bike is moving.

3. He is ________________ the handlebars.

4. He is ________________ his leg over the bike.

5. He is ________________ up his bike.

6. He is ________________ gears.

2. **Labeling** 올바른 단어 혹은 구를 〈보기〉에서 찾아서 쓰시오.

brakes
gears
handlebars
helmet
pedals
shift lever

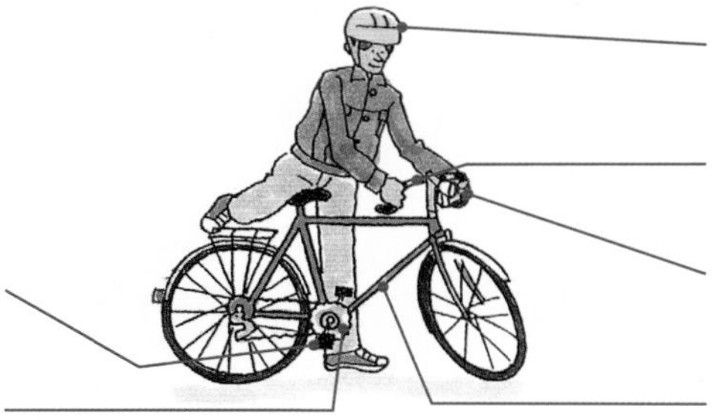

1. ________________
2. ________________
3. ________________
4. ________________
5. ________________
6. ________________

3. **Listening** (17) 다음을 듣고, 각 문항의 상황과 가장 어울리는 것 옆에 번호를 쓰시오.

______ a. The bike is slowing down.
______ b. She is not on a bike.
______ c. The bike is moving.
______ d. She is changing gears.
______ e. She has a helmet on.

Section

3

At Home in the Evening

Scan for Audio

DAY
18 Returning Home

1. Filling in 그림 아래의 빈칸에 올바른 단어 혹은 구를 〈보기〉에서 찾아서 쓰시오. 〈보기〉의 단어 혹은 구는 한 번만 사용하시오.

getting pressing taking hanging setting walking

1. He is ________________ down the hall to his apartment.

2. He is ________________ back to his house.

3. He is ________________ an elevator to his floor.

4. He is ________________ his bag down.

5. He is ________________ his coat up.

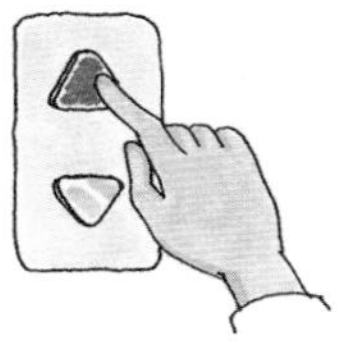

6. He is ________________ a button.

2. Matching 가장 올바른 설명을 B열에서 찾아서 A열 옆에 쓰시오.

	A	B
____	1. doorknob	a. a narrow passage that leads to other rooms
____	2. mailbox	b. you check this to see if you have any letters
____	3. building	c. many apartments can be inside this
____	4. closet	d. you can turn this to open a door
____	5. hall	e. you can hang coats here

3. Listening 18 다음을 듣고, 각 문항의 상황과 가장 어울리는 것 옆에 번호를 쓰시오.

_____ a. He is changing clothes.
_____ b. He is on an elevator.
_____ c. He lives in an apartment building, not a house.
_____ d. He is opening a door.
_____ e. He is on the steps.

DAY

19 Preparing Vegetables

1. **Filling in** 그림 아래의 빈칸에 올바른 단어 혹은 구를 〈보기〉에서 찾아서 쓰시오. 〈보기〉의 단어 혹은 구는 한 번만 사용하시오.

boiling   peeling   steaming   mixing   slicing   throwing

1. Someone is ________________ a carrot.

2. Someone is ________________ a carrot.

3. Someone is ________________ away broccoli stalks.

4. Someone is ________________ some lettuce and cucumbers.

5. The water is ________________.

6. The boiling water is ________________ the vegetables.

2. **Matching** 가장 올바른 설명을 B열에서 찾아서 A열 옆에 쓰시오.

	A	B
____	1. water	a. for rinsing things
____	2. grater	b. for cutting cucumbers or tomatoes
____	3. colander	c. for mixing and serving salad
____	4. knife	d. for draining lettuce
____	5. salad bowl	e. for shredding carrots into very small pieces

3. **Listening** (19) 다음을 듣고, 언급된 단어 혹은 구를 고르시오.

1. stalk	water	saucepan
2. lit	put	lid
3. light	inside	slice
4. chopped	broccoli	stalk
5. saucepan	basket	carrot

Making Spaghetti

1. **Filling in** 그림 아래의 빈칸에 올바른 단어 혹은 구를 〈보기〉에서 찾아서 쓰시오. 〈보기〉의 단어 혹은 구는 한 번만 사용하시오.

boiling	frying	pouring	dicing	ladling	stirring

1. Someone is ________________ off some fat.

2. The sauce is ________________.

3. Someone is ________________ sauce over some noodles.

4. Someone is ________________ an onion.

5. Someone is ________________ an onion and ground beef.

6. Someone is ________________ spice into some sauce.

2. **Matching** 가장 올바른 설명을 B열에서 찾아서 A열 옆에 쓰시오.

A	B
____ 1. spaghetti	a. a kind of pasta
____ 2. can	b. to make water go out of something
____ 3. simmer	c. to cook a liquid slowly and gently
____ 4. drain	d. this contains more than one part
____ 5. mixture	e. sauce can come from this

3. **Listening** (20) 다음을 듣고, 문장을 완성할 수 있는 가장 올바른 답을 고르시오.

1. The spaghetti is _______.	boiling	draining	frying
2. She is _______ something to the sauce.	adding	stirring	pouring
3. He is turning something _______.	off	over	down
4. The spaghetti has become _______.	tender	liquid	solid
5. He's putting something into a _______.	frying pan	saucepan	can

DAY

21 Cooking Rice

1. **Filling in** 그림 아래의 빈칸에 올바른 단어 혹은 구를 〈보기〉에서 찾아서 쓰시오. 〈보기〉의 단어 혹은 구는 한 번만 사용하시오.

spooning	rinsing	measuring	getting rid of	pouring	boiling

1. He is ________________ some rice onto his plate.

2. He is ________________ out a cup of rice.

3. He is ________________ the rice.

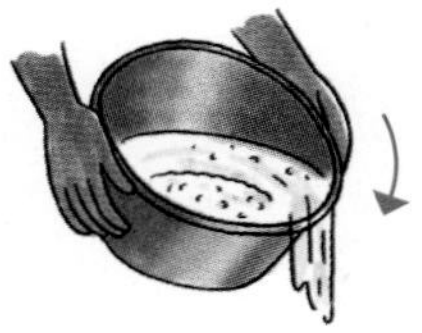

4. He is ________________ the dirt and husks in the rice.

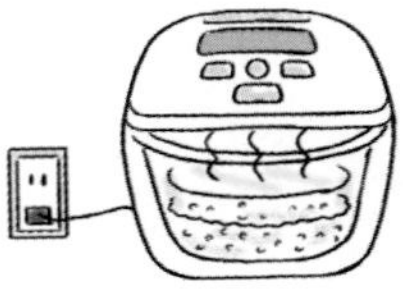

5. The rice is ________________ in the cooker.

6. He is ________________ rice into a pot.

2. **Matching** 가장 올바른 설명을 B열에서 찾아서 A열 옆에 쓰시오.

A	B
____ 1. lid	a. this is used to measure amounts
____ 2. pot	b. this goes on top of a pot
____ 3. cup	c. you can cook rice in this
____ 4. husk	d. this is the skin around a grain of rice
____ 5. clean	e. this means "not dirty"

3. **Listening** 21 다음을 듣고, 각 문항의 상황과 가장 어울리는 것 옆에 번호를 쓰시오.

_____ a. Someone is getting an exact amount of rice.
_____ b. Someone is getting rid of something.
_____ c. Someone is adding water to the rice to wash it.
_____ d. Someone can eat the rice.
_____ e. Someone should turn down the flame.

Eating Dinner

DAY 22

1. **Filling in** 그림 아래의 빈칸에 올바른 단어 혹은 구를 〈보기〉에서 찾아서 쓰시오. 〈보기〉의 단어 혹은 구는 한 번만 사용하시오.

having **passing** **setting** **helping** **putting** **sitting**

1. They are ________________ the table.

2. They are ________________ down at the table.

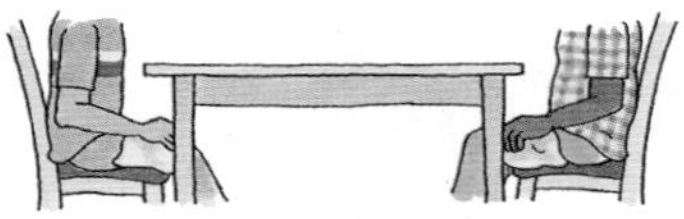

3. They are ________________ napkins on their laps.

4. He is ________________ himself to some food.

5. He is ________________ a second helping of food.

6. He is ________________ the serving dish.

2. **Labeling** 올바른 단어 혹은 구를 〈보기〉에서 찾아서 쓰시오.

coffee cup
fork
glass
knife
napkin
plate
spoon
salad bowl

1. ________________
2. ________________
3. ________________
4. ________________

5. ________________
6. ________________
7. ________________
8. ________________

3. **Listening** (22) 다음을 듣고, 문장을 완성할 수 있는 가장 올바른 답을 고르시오.

1. He is ______.	having dessert	setting the table	sitting
2. She has a ______.	helping	napkin	salad bowl
3. He will have ______.	dessert	salad	a second helping
4. She wants him to ______.	help himself	pass something	talk about something
5. He is ______.	eating	helping himself	setting the table

DAY 23 Cleaning Up

1. **Filling in** 그림 아래의 빈칸에 올바른 단어 혹은 구를 〈보기〉에서 찾아서 쓰시오. 〈보기〉의 단어 혹은 구는 한 번만 사용하시오.

carrying **scraping** **throwing** **offering** **stacking** **wiping**

1. They are ________________ to clear up.

2. Someone is ________________ the scraps from the plate.

3. He is ________________ the dishes to the kitchen.

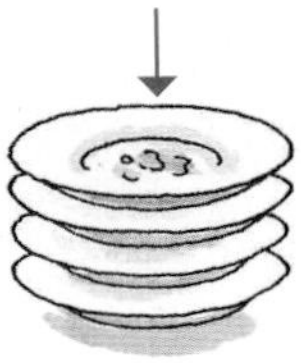

4. Someone is ________________ up some dishes.

5. Someone is ________________ the scraps into the garbage.

6. Someone is ________________ the table.

2. **Matching** 가장 올바른 설명을 B열에서 찾아서 A열 옆에 쓰시오.

A	B
____ 1. leftovers	a. food that people did not eat; you keep these in the refrigerator
____ 2. crumbs	b. this is like a small box; you can store food in it
____ 3. container	c. small pieces of meat, fruit, or other food that people didn't eat; you throw these away
____ 4. refrigerator	d. a machine that keeps things cold
____ 5. scraps	e. very small pieces of bread; you throw these away

3. **Listening** (23) 다음을 듣고, 언급된 단어 혹은 구를 고르시오.

1. pull the plug	put the plug	cupboard
2. pull the plug	put the plug	cupboard
3. wet dishes	water dripped	dirty dishes
4. rinsed	washed	towel
5. dishes	dish soap	rinsed

Using the Internet

DAY 24

1. Filling in 그림 아래의 빈칸에 올바른 단어 혹은 구를 〈보기〉에서 찾아서 쓰시오. 〈보기〉의 단어 혹은 구는 한 번만 사용하시오.

added	clicked	read	turned	typed	went

1. He ________________ his laptop on.

2. He ________________ in his username and password.

3. He ________________ on his browser to go to the Internet.

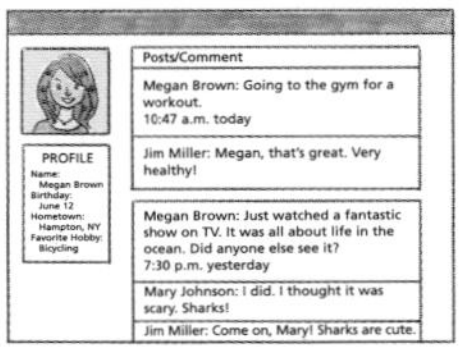

4. He ________________ to his friend's page at a social networking site.

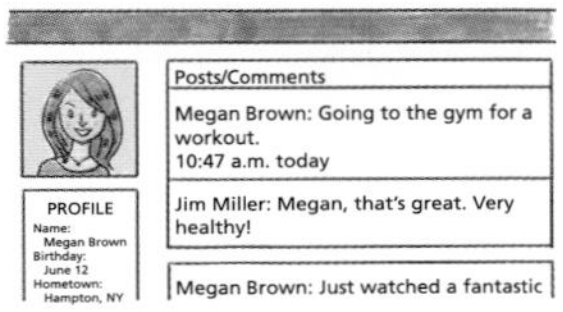

5. He ________________ some posts on her page.

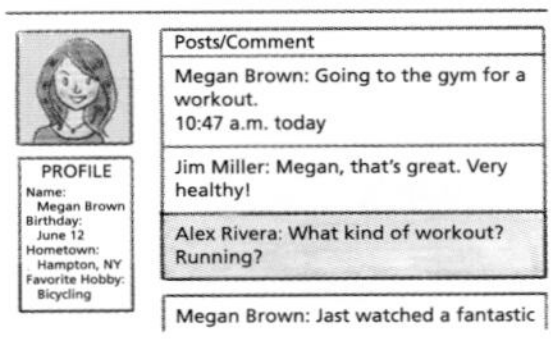

6. He ________________ a comment on her page.

2. Matching 가장 올바른 설명을 B열에서 찾아서 A열 옆에 쓰시오.

A	B
____ 1. browser	a. a kind of computer
____ 2. keys	b. a place to connect a USB cable
____ 3. laptop	c. these are used when you type
____ 4. password	d. it helps you get on the Internet
____ 5. port	e. this is entered when you log on

3. Listening (24) 다음을 듣고, 언급된 단어 혹은 구를 고르시오.

1. laptop	logged on	comment
2. video	Internet	clicked
3. social networking	USB port	some posts
4. address	added	mousepad
5. typed	page	site

DAY 25

Listening to Music

1. Filling in 그림 아래의 빈칸에 올바른 단어 혹은 구를 〈보기〉에서 찾아서 쓰시오. 〈보기〉의 단어 혹은 구는 한 번만 사용하시오.

connected   selected   held   looked through   tapped   adjusted

1. He ________________ his earphones to his phone.

2. He ________________ the volume by pressing the button.

3. He ________________ the screen to play a song.

4. He ________________ his music and found a playlist.

5. He ________________ his music application.

6. He ________________ the button and turned off his phone.

2. Matching 가장 올바른 설명을 B열에서 찾아서 A열 옆에 쓰시오.

A	B
____ 1. adjust	a. a swinging movement of your hands or fingers
____ 2. swipe	b. loudness
____ 3. screen	c. a list of choices
____ 4. volume	d. to change something to make it better
____ 5. menu	e. the part of a media player that shows pictures, words, etc.

3. Listening (25) 다음을 듣고, 문장을 완성할 수 있는 가장 올바른 답을 고르시오.

1. The music got ______.	smaller	louder	softer
2. Alex ______ his screen.	played	selected	swiped
3. Alex ______ his earphones.	swiped	connected	tapped
4. Alex ______ his screen.	selected	pressed	tapped
5. There were icons for many ______.	apps	buttons	screens

Reading

1. Filling in 그림 아래의 빈칸에 올바른 단어 혹은 구를 〈보기〉에서 찾아서 쓰시오. 〈보기〉의 단어 혹은 구는 한 번만 사용하시오.

closing	looking at	looking up	opening	reading	turning

1. She has finished reading the book and is __________ it.

2. She is __________ the pages as she reads.

3. She is __________ an article in a magazine.

4. She is __________ a word in a dictionary.

5. She is __________ the pictures in a magazine.

6. She is __________ a magazine.

3. Labeling 올바른 단어 혹은 구를 〈보기〉에서 찾아서 쓰시오.

보기
author's name
caption
cover
page number
table of contents
title

1. __________
2. __________
3. __________
4. __________

5. __________
6. __________

3. Listening (26) 다음을 듣고, 문장을 완성할 수 있는 가장 올바른 답을 고르시오.

1. She is ______ something.	looking up	flipping through	looking at
2. He is reading words that are ______.	next to a picture	in an index	in a table of contents
3. She is looking at a ______.	cover	bookmark	table of contents
4. He has ______ an interesting article.	opened	finished	found
5. She has ______ reading.	finished	closed	looked up

DAY
27 Watching Television

1. **Filling in** 그림 아래의 빈칸에 올바른 단어 혹은 구를 〈보기〉에서 찾아서 쓰시오. 〈보기〉의 단어 혹은 구는 한 번만 사용하시오.

changing **turning off** **turning up** **ending** **turning on** **watching**

1. He is __________________ the volume.

2. The news is __________________.

3. He is __________________ the news on TV.

4. He is __________________ the TV.

5. He is __________________ the TV.

6. He is __________________ channels.

2. **Matching** 가장 올바른 설명을 B열에서 찾아서 A열 옆에 쓰시오.

A	B
_____ 1. boring	a. you use this to change channels
_____ 2. commercials	b. not interesting
_____ 3. news	c. a report about things that have happened
_____ 4. remote	d. something to eat
_____ 5. snack	e. advertising on TV

3. **Listening** (27) 다음을 듣고, 언급된 단어 혹은 구를 고르시오.

1. snack	channel	show
2. change channels	game show	commercial
3. volume	remote	show
4. was on	watched	went
5. turned it up	turned it on	turned it off

DAY 28

Streaming Services

1. **Filling in** 그림 아래의 빈칸에 올바른 단어 혹은 구를 〈보기〉에서 찾아서 쓰시오. 〈보기〉의 단어 혹은 구는 한 번만 사용하시오.

searched	browsed	changed	subscribed	went	watched

1. Jenny ________________ through the streaming service's new releases.

2. She ________________ to the vlogger's channel.

3. She ________________ to a different streaming service.

4. She ________________ for her favorite vlogger.

5. She ________________ the vlogger's livestream.

6. Jenny ________________ to her favorite streaming service.

2. **Matching** 가장 올바른 설명을 B열에서 찾아서 A열 옆에 쓰시오.

	A	B
____	1. browse	a. a continuing flow of data or information
____	2. chat	b. to talk with someone
____	3. subscribe	c. a person who posts short videos about their interests or life
____	4. vlogger	d. to sign up to get something regularly
____	5. stream	e. to look through many things

3. **Listening** (28) 다음을 듣고, 언급된 단어 혹은 구를 고르시오.

1. searched	watched	browsed
2. subscribed	streaming	vlogger
3. finish	chatted	picked
4. searched	subscribed	service
5. notification	vlogger	livestream

DAY 29 Going to Bed

1. **Filling in** 그림 아래의 빈칸에 올바른 단어 혹은 구를 〈보기〉에서 찾아서 쓰시오. 〈보기〉의 단어 혹은 구는 한 번만 사용하시오.

getting	hanging	setting	going	lying	yawning

1. She is __________ down.

2. She is __________ upstairs.

3. She is __________ her alarm clock.

4. She is __________ into bed.

5. She is __________ up some of her clothes.

6. She is __________.

2. **Matching** 가장 올바른 설명을 B열에서 찾아서 A열 옆에 쓰시오..

	A	B
____	1. bedside lamp	a. you can put a lamp or a clock on this
____	2. closet	b. a place to hang clothes
____	3. covers	c. sheets and blankets on a bed
____	4. nightstand	d. you can walk up these
____	5. stairs	e. this gives light

3. **Listening** (29) 다음을 듣고, 각 문항의 상황과 가장 어울리는 것 옆에 번호를 쓰시오.

_____ a. Someone is yawning.
_____ b. Someone is saying goodnight.
_____ c. The room is dark.
_____ d. Someone is sitting on the bed and looking through a book.
_____ e. Someone has put on clothes for bed.

Memo

Section

4

Managing a Household

Scan for Audio

DAY
30

Doing Laundry

1. Filling in 그림 아래의 빈칸에 올바른 단어 혹은 구를 〈보기〉에서 찾아서 쓰시오. 〈보기〉의 단어 혹은 구는 한 번만 사용하시오.

checking	folding	sorting	drying	spinning	washing

1. The washing machine is ________________ the laundry.

2. The clothes are ________________ in the sun.

3. The machine is ________________ the laundry.

4. He is ________________ the pockets.

5. He is ________________ the laundry.

6. He is ________________ some clothes.

2. Matching 가장 올바른 설명을 B열에서 찾아서 A열 옆에 쓰시오.

	A	B
____	1. clothesline	a. clothes that are being washed
____	2. dryer	b. a machine that can wash, rinse, and spin
____	3. iron	c. a machine that uses heat and tumbles the laundry
____	4. laundry	d. a tool for making washed clothes smooth
____	5. washer	e. a place to hang wet laundry so it will dry

3. Listening 30 다음을 듣고, 각 문항의 상황과 가장 어울리는 것 옆에 번호를 쓰시오.

______ a. Someone is turning the controls.
______ b. Someone is adding soap.
______ c. The laundry is wet.
______ d. The laundry is dry.
______ e. Someone is carrying dirty laundry.

DAY 31

Cleaning the House

1. Filling in 그림 아래의 빈칸에 올바른 단어 혹은 구를 〈보기〉에서 찾아서 쓰시오. 〈보기〉의 단어 혹은 구는 한 번만 사용하시오.

throwing	scrubbing	wiping	mopping	sweeping	vacuuming

1. She is _______________ the floor.

2. He is _______________ the floor.

3. He is _______________ out the spoiled food.

4. She is _______________ the countertops in the kitchen.

5. He is _______________ the toilet with a brush.

6. She is _______________ the carpet.

3. Labeling 올바른 단어 혹은 구를 〈보기〉에서 찾아서 쓰시오.

broom
bucket
dustpan
garbage bag
garbage can
wastebasket

1. _______________
2. _______________

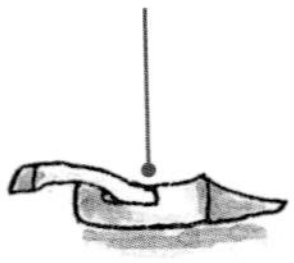

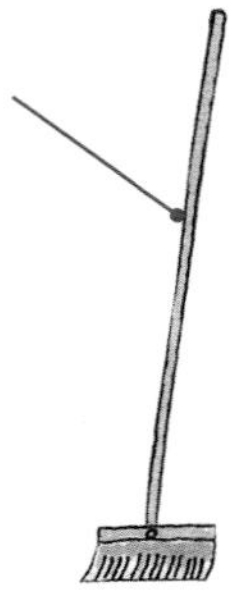

3. _______________

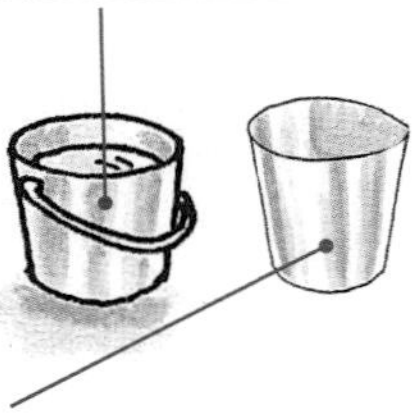

4. _______________

5. _______________

6. _______________

3. Listening 31 다음을 듣고, 문장을 완성할 수 있는 가장 올바른 답을 고르시오.

1. He is _______ something out.
2. She is _______ things.
3. He is cleaning the _______.
4. She is cleaning the _______.
5. He is working with _______.

throwing	setting	cleaning
bundling	emptying	recycling
kitchen	bathroom	living room
furniture	floor	refrigerator
bottles	newspapers	food

Taking Care of Pets

1. Filling in 그림 아래의 빈칸에 올바른 단어 혹은 구를 〈보기〉에서 찾아서 쓰시오. 〈보기〉의 단어 혹은 구는 한 번만 사용하시오.

cleaning **petting** **purring** **feeding** **playing** **putting**

1. The cat is ________________ with a piece of string.

2. He is ________________ his cat.

3. He is ________________ his cat.

4. He is ________________ fresh water into the water dish.

5. He is ________________ the litter box.

6. The cat is ________________.

2. Matching 가장 올바른 설명을 B열에서 찾아서 A열 옆에 쓰시오.

A	B
____ 1. collar	a. this clips to a collar
____ 2. dish	b. a part of a dog's body
____ 3. leash	c. this goes around a dog's neck
____ 4. stick	d. it can contain water or food
____ 5. tail	e. a dog fetches this

3. Listening (32) 다음을 듣고, 언급된 단어 혹은 구를 고르시오.

1. putting	purring	playing
2. dish	fresh	litter
3. can	cat	clean
4. petting	putting	purring
5. opened	box	pounced

DAY 33

Cleaning a Car

1. **Filling in** 그림 아래의 빈칸에 올바른 단어 혹은 구를 〈보기〉에서 찾아서 쓰시오. 〈보기〉의 단어 혹은 구는 한 번만 사용하시오.

dipping   rinsing   washing   drying   spreading   wiping

1. She is ________________ off the dashboard with a dry cloth.

2. She is ________________ wax on the car.

3. She is ________________ the car.

4. She is ________________ the car with soapy water.

5. She is ________________ the car with some rags.

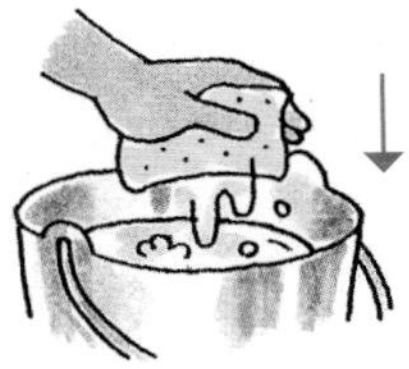

6. She is ________________ a sponge into soapy water.

2. **Matching** 가장 올바른 설명을 B열에서 찾아서 A열 옆에 쓰시오.

	A	B
____	1. bucket	a. a kind of cloth
____	2. dashboard	b. it can be used for washing; it has a lot of holes in it
____	3. rag	c. a part of the inside of a car
____	4. sponge	d. this can be spread on a car to make it shine
____	5. wax	e. this holds water

3. **Listening** 다음을 듣고, 각 문항의 상황과 가장 어울리는 것 옆에 번호를 쓰시오.

_____ a. Someone is moving a cloth quickly back and forth to make the car shine.
_____ b. Someone is cleaning the inside of a car.
_____ c. Someone is using water.
_____ d. Someone is using wax.
_____ e. Someone is cleaning windows.

Taking a Car to a Garage for Repairs

DAY 34

1. **Filling in** 그림 아래의 빈칸에 올바른 단어 혹은 구를 〈보기〉에서 찾아서 쓰시오. 〈보기〉의 단어 혹은 구는 한 번만 사용하시오.

asking **coming** **taking** **calling** **giving** **working**

1. He is ________________ his car in for repairs.

2. The mechanic is ________________ on the car.

3. He is ________________ the mechanic for an estimate.

4. The mechanic is ________________ him the bill.

5. He is ________________ the garage.

6. He is ________________ back to get his car.

2. **Matching** 가장 올바른 설명을 B열에서 찾아서 A열 옆에 쓰시오.

A	B
____ 1. bill	a. a guess about an amount
____ 2. engine	b. a piece of paper saying how much you must pay
____ 3. estimate	c. a place where cars get fixed
____ 4. garage	d. a person who fixes cars
____ 5. mechanic	e. a part of a car

3. **Listening** (34) 다음을 듣고, 문장을 완성할 수 있는 가장 올바른 답을 고르시오.

1. He is ______.	calling	diagnosing	estimating
2. She wants to ______ her car.	pick up	work on	take in
3. He is asking for ______.	repairs	an estimate	a bill
4. She will ______.	fix her car	get her car fixed	work on the engine
5. He is ______.	calling	diagnosing	estimating

DAY
35 Shopping for Groceries

1. **Filling in** 그림 아래의 빈칸에 올바른 단어 혹은 구를 〈보기〉에서 찾아서 쓰시오. 〈보기〉의 단어 혹은 구는 한 번만 사용하시오.

choosing   putting   trying   going   taking   weighing

1. He is ________________ the fruit.

2. He is ________________ a free sample.

3. He is ________________ fruit into a bag.

4. He is ________________ something out.

5. He is ________________ through an aisle.

6. He is ________________ the cheaper peas.

2. **Matching** 가장 올바른 설명을 B열에서 찾아서 A열 옆에 쓰시오.

A	B
____ 1. special	a. something that is at a lower price than usual
____ 2. section	b. to look quickly at something to make sure it's okay
____ 3. check	c. a part of a store (or of some other thing)
____ 4. pick up	d. to get something while you're shopping
____ 5. checkout counter	e. a place where you pay for your groceries

3. **Listening** (35) 다음을 듣고, 각 문항의 상황과 가장 어울리는 것 옆에 번호를 쓰시오.

____ a. He's reading a list.
____ b. She's picking up some cheese.
____ c. He's picking up some cold cuts.
____ d. She's picking up some fresh meat.
____ e. He's in the dairy section.
____ f. She's in the fresh produce section.

Paying for Things

1. Filling in 그림 아래의 빈칸에 올바른 단어 혹은 구를 〈보기〉에서 찾아서 쓰시오. 〈보기〉의 단어 혹은 구는 한 번만 사용하시오.

inserting **signing** **scanning** **pressing** **counting** **unlocking**

1. She is __________ change.

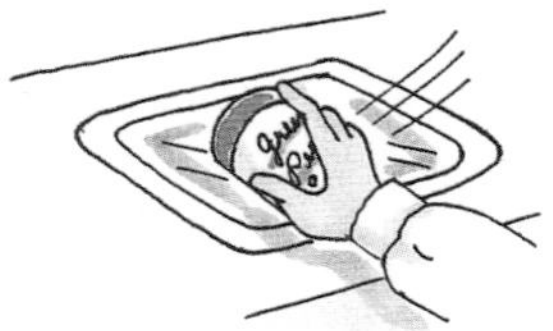

2. She is __________ a bar code.

3. He is __________ his phone to pay.

4. She is __________ the keys.

5. He is __________ the card reader.

6. She is __________ the card into the reader.

2. Matching 가장 올바른 설명을 B열에서 찾아서 A열 옆에 쓰시오.

	A	B
____	1. code	a. a kind of machine
____	2. change	b. a piece of paper, listing purchases
____	3. receipt	c. a set of letters or numbers
____	4. cash register	d. money given back to a customer
____	5. wallet	e. a place to keep money that is not a machine

3. Listening (36) 다음을 듣고, 각 문항의 상황과 가장 어울리는 것 옆에 번호를 쓰시오.

_____ a. He's asking to pay with his phone.
_____ b. He's paying money.
_____ c. He's counting out some change.
_____ d. Someone has scanned a bar code.
_____ e. He's telling someone the total to pay.
_____ f. He's paying by credit card.

DAY
37 Going to the Bank

1. Filling in 그림 아래의 빈칸에 올바른 단어 혹은 구를 〈보기〉에서 찾아서 쓰시오. 〈보기〉의 단어 혹은 구는 한 번만 사용하시오.

checking   filling out   going   endorsing   giving   printing

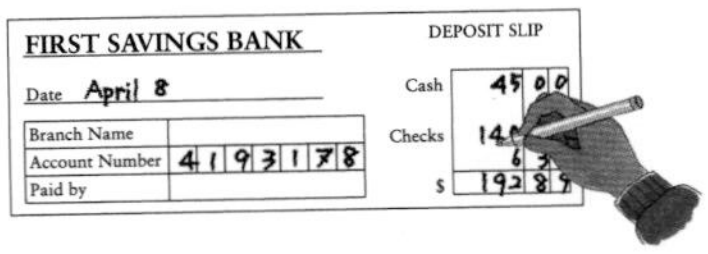

1. He is ________________ a deposit slip.

2. The teller is ________________ the amounts.

Transaction	Amount	Balance
Carried forward		1221.64
Deposit	192.89	1414.53

3. A machine is ________________ the amount in his passbook.

4. He is ________________ to the bank.

5. He is ________________ a check by signing it on the back.

6. The teller is ________________ back his passbook.

2. Matching 가장 올바른 설명을 B열에서 찾아서 A열 옆에 쓰시오.

A	B
____ 1. account	a. the result of adding several amounts of money
____ 2. counter	b. a bank's record of someone's money in the bank
____ 3. deposit slip	c. a place in a bank where you can fill out deposit slips
____ 4. teller	d. a piece of paper
____ 5. total	e. someone who works at a bank

3. Listening (37) 다음을 듣고, 문장을 완성할 수 있는 가장 올바른 답을 고르시오.

1. He's ______ something.	endorsing	filling out	checking
2. She's finding the ______.	window	account	total
3. He's saying his ______.	total	name	account number
4. She's standing at a ______.	passbook	slip	window
5. He's giving someone ______.	a check	some cash	a teller

Memo

Section

5

Keeping in Touch

Scan for Audio

DAY 38 Getting and Sending Email

1. **Filling in** 그림 아래의 빈칸에 올바른 단어 혹은 구를 〈보기〉에서 찾아서 쓰시오. 〈보기〉의 단어 혹은 구는 한 번만 사용하시오.

clicked	log in	opened	printed	replied to	deleted

1. Alex ________________ on his browser to go online.

2. He typed in his username and password to ________________.

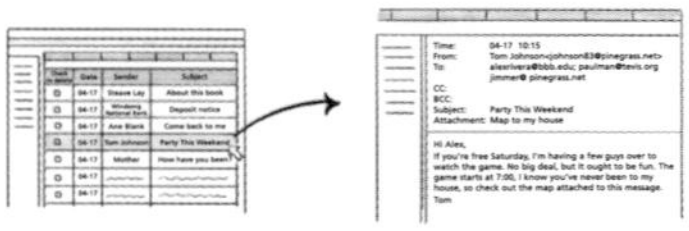

3. To read an email message, he ________________ it.

4. He ________________ the message by writing back to the sender.

5. He ________________ out an attachment.

6. He ________________ a message, which means he sent it to the trash.

2. **Matching** 가장 올바른 설명을 B열에서 찾아서 A열 옆에 쓰시오.

	A	B
_____	1. attachment	a. something (a picture, text, etc.) that you send along with an email message
_____	2. date	b. unwanted email messages that are sent to lots of people
_____	3. mailbox	c. the day when an email is sent
_____	4. recipient	d. the place in an email program where incoming messages go
_____	5. spam	e. the person who receives an email message

3. **Listening** (38) 다음을 듣고, 언급된 단어 혹은 구를 고르시오.

1. clicked	printed	into
2. typed	online	replied
3. password	address	attachment
4. click on	icon	typed on
5. deleted	received	email

DAY 39
Using a Mobile Phone / Texting

1. Filling in 그림 아래의 빈칸에 올바른 단어 혹은 구를 〈보기〉에서 찾아서 쓰시오. 〈보기〉의 단어 혹은 구는 한 번만 사용하시오.

answered dialed pick up shined texted took

1. Dan ________________ a number to make a call.

2. The other person didn't ________________ the phone.

3. Jim ________________ a call from Dan.

4. Pam ________________ her friend on her cell phone; she did not talk to her friend.

5. Dan ________________ a light.

6. Dan ________________ a picture with his cell phone.

2. Matching 가장 올바른 설명을 B열에서 찾아서 A열 옆에 쓰시오.

A	B
____ 1. abbreviations	a. to send someone a short message to their phone
____ 2. contact	b. short forms of phrases, such as "BRB" for "be right back"
____ 3. emoticon	c. the sound a cell phone makes when you get a call
____ 4. text	d. a symbol that is supposed to look like a face
____ 5. ringtone	e. someone whose number is listed in your cell phone

3. Listening (39) 다음을 듣고, 언급된 단어 혹은 구를 고르시오.

1. ended	sent	went
2. selected "Text"	sent messages	pressed "Send"
3. texted	pressed	shined
4. shine	write	find
5. hitting	did things	listing

DAY 40

Making a Phone Call

1. Filling in 그림 아래의 빈칸에 올바른 단어 혹은 구를 〈보기〉에서 찾아서 쓰시오. 〈보기〉의 단어 혹은 구는 한 번만 사용하시오.

answering identifying picking up dialing looking up unlocking

1. She is __________ herself.

2. She is __________ the phone.

3. She is __________ a number.

4. She is __________ a number.

5. She is __________ the phone.

6. She is __________ the telephone.

2. Matching 가장 올바른 설명을 B열에서 찾아서 A열 옆에 쓰시오.

A	B
____ 1. dial	a. to take a phone call
____ 2. answer	b. you dial this to call someone
____ 3. look up	c. to make a sound
____ 4. phone number	d. to search for something
____ 5. ring	e. to make a phone call

3. Listening 40 다음을 듣고, 각 문항의 상황과 가장 어울리는 것 옆에 번호를 쓰시오.

_____ a. The phone is ringing.
_____ b. Someone is answering the phone.
_____ c. Someone is saying why he called.
_____ d. Someone is identifying herself.
_____ e. Someone is dialing a number.

DAY
41 Answering a Telephone

1. **Filling in** 그림 아래의 빈칸에 올바른 단어 혹은 구를 〈보기〉에서 찾아서 쓰시오. 〈보기〉의 단어 혹은 구는 한 번만 사용하시오.

answering **hanging up** **talking** **apologizing** **taking** **telling**

1. She is ________________ him he has a wrong number.

2. She is ________________ the phone.

3. They are ________________ on the phone.

4. She is ________________.

5. She is ________________ the phone off the charger.

6. He is ________________ for calling the wrong number.

2. **Matching** 가장 올바른 설명을 B열에서 찾아서 A열 옆에 쓰시오.

A	B
____ 1. caller	a. one way of answering a phone
____ 2. let someone speak	b. when you do this, you stay silent
____ 3. hang up	c. not the phone number you wanted to call
____ 4. saying hello	d. the person who makes a phone call
____ 5. wrong number	e. you do this to end a phone call

3. **Listening** 41 다음을 듣고, 각 문항의 상황과 가장 어울리는 것 옆에 번호를 쓰시오.

_____ a. Someone is answering the phone.

_____ b. Some people are talking on the phone.

_____ c. Someone is asking to speak to another person.

_____ d. Someone is telling a caller he or she has a wrong number.

_____ e. Someone is apologizing.

Leaving a Message

DAY 42

1. Filling in 그림 아래의 빈칸에 올바른 단어 혹은 구를 〈보기〉에서 찾아서 쓰시오. 〈보기〉의 단어 혹은 구는 한 번만 사용하시오.

agreeing	identifying	spelling	asking	leaving	repeating

1. She is ________________ to take a message.

2. He is ________________ his name.

3. He is ________________ his name.

4. He is ________________ a message.

5. He is ________________ himself.

6. He is ________________ to leave a message.

2. Matching 가장 올바른 설명을 B열에서 찾아서 A열 옆에 쓰시오.

A	B
____ 1. available	a. the word "Tom" in "Tom Smith"
____ 2. first name	b. the word "Smith" in "Tom Smith"
____ 3. last name	c. able to see you or speak with you
____ 4. message	d. to say again
____ 5. repeat	e. information you want to give to someone

3. Listening 42 다음을 듣고, 각 문항의 상황과 가장 어울리는 것 옆에 번호를 쓰시오.

_____ a. Someone is asking to speak to someone else.
_____ b. Someone is asking that someone else call back.
_____ c. Someone is repeating something.
_____ d. Someone is spelling something.
_____ e. Someone is leaving a number.

DAY
43 Taking a Message

1. Filling in 그림 아래의 빈칸에 올바른 단어 혹은 구를 〈보기〉에서 찾아서 쓰시오. 〈보기〉의 단어 혹은 구는 한 번만 사용하시오.

answering	returning	leaving	asking	offering	writing

1. She is ________________ a message on some notepaper.

2. She is ________________ to take a message.

3. He is ________________ for someone.

4. He is ________________ someone's call.

5. He is ________________ a message.

6. She is ________________ the phone.

2. Listening 1 (43) 다음을 듣고, 문장을 완성할 수 있는 가장 올바른 답을 고르시오.

1. Bob left a message ______ Karen.	about	for	next to	on	with
2. Bob left a message ______ Ted.	about	for	next to	on	with
3. Karen wrote a message ______ notepaper.	about	for	next to	on	with
4. Karen left a message ______ the phone.	about	for	next to	on	with
5. Bob left a message ______ basketball.	about	for	next to	on	with

3. Listening 2 (44) 다음을 듣고, 각 문항의 상황과 가장 어울리는 것 옆에 번호를 쓰시오.

______ a. Someone is answering the phone.
______ b. Someone is asking for a particular person.
______ c. Someone is returning a call.
______ d. Someone is leaving a message.
______ e. Someone is offering to take a message.

Video Conferencing

DAY 44

1. Filling in 그림 아래의 빈칸에 올바른 단어 혹은 구를 〈보기〉에서 찾아서 쓰시오. 〈보기〉의 단어 혹은 구는 한 번만 사용하시오.

answered	testing	discussing	turning on	selecting	sharing

1. Dan is ________________ his video conferencing application.

2. Tom is ________________ his screen with the group.

3. Dan is ________________ his webcam.

4. Dan is ________________ people on his contact list.

5. They are ________________ their work as a group.

6. Tom and Pam get the invite and ________________.

2. Matching 가장 올바른 설명을 B열에서 찾아서 A열 옆에 쓰시오.

	A	B
____	1. webcam	a. equipment used to input or record someone's voice
____	2. microphone	b. there are many icons on this
____	3. connection	c. equipment used with a computer to film video
____	4. screen	d. a machine or equipment
____	5. device	e. this is needed to be on the Internet

3. Listening 45 다음을 듣고, 언급된 단어 혹은 구를 고르시오.

1. allowing	sending	testing
2. inviting	testing	selecting
3. discussing	sharing	sending
4. chatting	inviting	discussing
5. sharing	allowing	answering

DAY
45 Posting on Social Media

1. **Filling in** 그림 아래의 빈칸에 올바른 단어 혹은 구를 〈보기〉에서 찾아서 쓰시오. 〈보기〉의 단어 혹은 구는 한 번만 사용하시오.

adding	writing	looking	uploading	opening	commenting

1. Jenny is ________________ a social media application.

2. Jenny is ________________ effects and a filter.

3. She is ________________ a message on the photo.

4. She is ________________ on her friend's post.

5. She is ________________ a photo to share with her friends.

6. Jenny is ________________ at a photo of her and her friends.

2. **Matching** 가장 올바른 설명을 B열에서 찾아서 A열 옆에 쓰시오.

A

____ 1. discussion
____ 2. effect
____ 3. feed
____ 4. post
____ 5. comment

B

a. talking about something with another person or group
b. to put online
c. an online broadcast of content
d. something added to change and improve an image
e. to write a message on social media

3. **Listening** (46) 다음을 듣고, 언급된 단어 혹은 구를 고르시오.

1. posting	commenting	adding
2. commenting	posting	writing
3. adding	checking	commenting
4. checking	adding	feeding
5. commenting	leaving	adding

Mailing a Letter

DAY 46

1. Filling in 그림 아래의 빈칸에 올바른 단어 혹은 구를 〈보기〉에서 찾아서 쓰시오. 〈보기〉의 단어 혹은 구는 한 번만 사용하시오.

enclosing	licking	sticking	folding	sealing	writing

1. He is ________________ up a letter.

2. He is ________________ some pictures.

3. He is ________________ the envelope.

4. He is ________________ a stamp.

5. He is ________________ the address on an envelope.

6. He is ________________ stamps on an envelope.

2. Matching 가장 올바른 설명을 B열에서 찾아서 A열 옆에 쓰시오.

A	B
____ 1. envelope	a. a box for sending or receiving letters
____ 2. line	b. you can seal this after you put a letter in it
____ 3. mailbox	c. a place where you can buy stamps
____ 4. post office	d. after you buy this, you stick it on an envelope
____ 5. stamp	e. you stand in this until it's your turn

3. Listening (47) 다음을 듣고, 각 문항의 상황과 가장 어울리는 것 옆에 번호를 쓰시오.

_____ a. Someone is weighing a letter.
_____ b. Someone wants a letter delivered in a faster, more expensive way.
_____ c. Someone is waiting for her turn.
_____ d. Someone is buying stamps.
_____ e. Someone wants a letter delivered in the usual or normal way.

Section 6

Having Fun with Friends

Scan for Audio

DAY
47 Going to a Party

1. **Filling in** 그림 아래의 빈칸에 올바른 단어 혹은 구를 〈보기〉에서 찾아서 쓰시오. 〈보기〉의 단어 혹은 구는 한 번만 사용하시오.

blowing	lighting	singing	giving	signing	wrapping

1. He is __________ a present to his friend.

2. They are __________ "Happy Birthday."

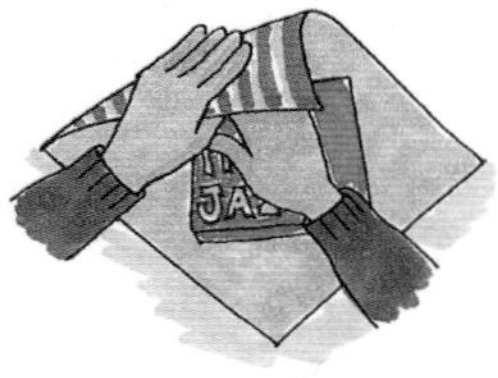

3. He is __________ a present.

4. He is __________ out the candles.

5. He is __________ the candles.

6. He is __________ a birthday card.

2. **Matching** 가장 올바른 설명을 B열에서 찾아서 A열 옆에 쓰시오.

	A	B
_____	1. match	a. you use this to light a candle
_____	2. present	b. the part of a candle that burns
_____	3. wax	c. the outside part of a candle
_____	4. wick	d. a gift
_____	5. wrapping paper	e. this goes around the outside of a present

3. **Listening** (48) 다음을 듣고, 언급된 단어 혹은 구를 고르시오.

1. blowing	opening	going
2. ice cream	lighting	sing
3. cake	present	birthday
4. sign	sing	light
5. happy	wrapping	candle

DAY
48 Going to a Movie

1. **Filling in** 그림 아래의 빈칸에 올바른 단어 혹은 구를 〈보기〉에서 찾아서 쓰시오. 〈보기〉의 단어 혹은 구는 한 번만 사용하시오.

buying **giving** **tearing** **finding** **going** **watching**

1. They are __________ tickets to a movie.

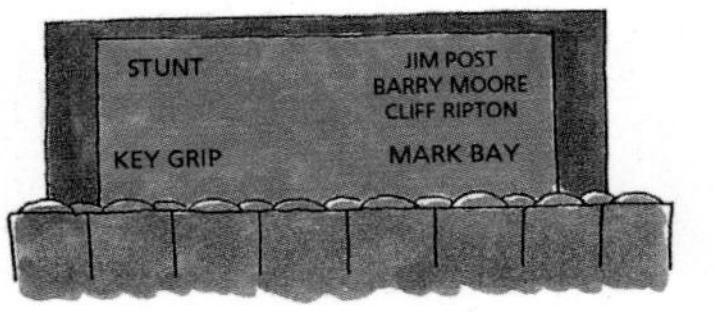

2. They are __________ the credits.

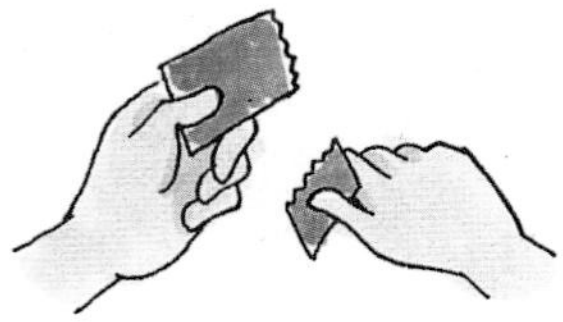

3. He is __________ the movie ticket.

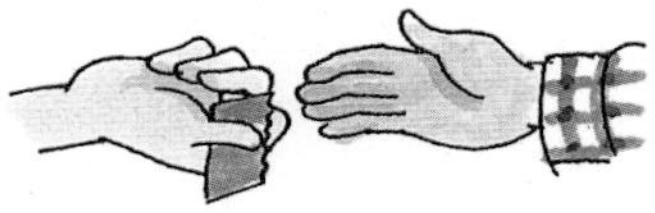

4. He is __________ the ticket stub back.

5. They are __________ to their seats.

6. He is __________ out which movies are showing.

2. **Matching** 가장 올바른 설명을 B열에서 찾아서 A열 옆에 쓰시오.

A

____ 1. box office
____ 2. credits
____ 3. popcorn
____ 4. preview
____ 5. stub

B

a. writing that says who worked on a movie
b. something people eat
c. a part of a movie shown that is not the main feature
d. a part of a ticket
e. a place to buy tickets

3. **Listening** (49) 다음을 듣고, 문장을 완성할 수 있는 가장 올바른 답을 고르시오.

1. They are buying _______.	tickets	popcorn	credits
2. They are watching _______.	a preview	the credits	the main feature
3. Someone _______ a ticket.	bought	sold	tore
4. The woman works at a _______.	snack counter	box office	coming attraction
5. She is talking about _______.	where the movie is showing	when the movie is showing	who worked on the movie

Eating at a Fast-Food Restaurant

DAY 49

1. **Filling in** 그림 아래의 빈칸에 올바른 단어 혹은 구를 〈보기〉에서 찾아서 쓰시오. 〈보기〉의 단어 혹은 구는 한 번만 사용하시오.

eating	paying	standing	ordering	reading	throwing

1. She is ________________ in line.

2. She is ________________ the menu.

3. She is ________________ lunch.

4. She is ________________ for her food.

5. She is ________________ her food.

6. She is ________________ an empty wrapper in the trash.

2. **Matching** 가장 올바른 설명을 B열에서 찾아서 A열 옆에 쓰시오.

A	B
____ 1. dispenser	a. you can get napkins and straws from these
____ 2. for here	b. to be eaten in the restaurant
____ 3. menu	c. to be eaten outside the restaurant
____ 4. to go	d. this lists the food you can buy at a restaurant
____ 5. wrapper	e. paper or boxes that go around food

3. **Listening** (50) 다음을 듣고, 각 문항의 상황과 가장 어울리는 것 옆에 번호를 쓰시오.

_____ a. Someone is throwing something away.
_____ b. Someone ordered food for here.
_____ c. Someone ordered food to go.
_____ d. Someone is ordering a drink.
_____ e. Someone is paying for food.

DAY 50

Having Coffee at a Coffee Shop

1. **Filling in** 그림 아래의 빈칸에 올바른 단어 혹은 구를 〈보기〉에서 찾아서 쓰시오. 〈보기〉의 단어 혹은 구는 한 번만 사용하시오.

drink plugged pumped ordered punched sat down

1. Pam and Jenny _______________ coffee at the counter.

2. They told the clerk they wanted their coffee "for here," to _______________ it in the coffee shop.

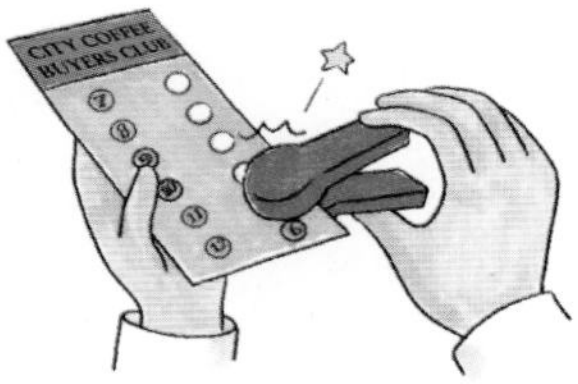

3. The clerk _______________ Jenny's frequent-customer card.

4. Pam _______________ some coffee out of the container.

5. They _______________ at a table.

6. Jenny _______________ her laptop into an outlet.

2. **Matching** 가장 올바른 설명을 B열에서 찾아서 A열 옆에 쓰시오.

A	B
____ 1. counter	a. a large cup
____ 2. espresso	b. wireless access to the Internet
____ 3. mug	c. the part of a shop where you order things
____ 4. refill	d. extra servings of coffee in the same cup
____ 5. Wi-Fi	e. strong coffee, usually served in a small cup

3. **Listening** 51 다음을 듣고, 언급된 단어 혹은 구를 고르시오.

1. the clerk	container	for here
2. was free	coffee	frequent
3. outlet	counter	called out
4. Internet	finished	muffin
5. pumped	empty	dirty

Memo

Transcript

Answer Key

Transcript

Day 1 Exercise III

1. It's seven o'clock. I should get up.
2. I'm just going to go into the shower.
3. I'm using a razor.
4. I'm drinking some coffee. And I'm having an egg and some toast.

Day 2 Exercise III

1. I'm flossing.
2. I'm done brushing, and now I'm putting my toothbrush away.
3. I'm spitting water into the sink.
4. I'm squeezing some toothpaste onto my toothbrush.

Day 3 Exercise III

1. I am washing all of my body.
2. I'm drying myself off.
3. I'm drying my hair.
4. I'm putting something under my arms to take away bad smells.

Day 4 Exercise III

1. Some shorts
2. Some socks
3. A button
4. A T-shirt
5. A cuff
6. Some shoes
7. Some underpants
8. Some laces
9. Some pants

Day 5 Exercise III

1. Some gloves
2. Some mittens
3. A blouse
4. A bra
5. A dress
6. A skirt

Day 6 Exercise III

1. I'm spreading a bedspread over the bed.
2. I'm putting a new pillowcase over this pillow.
3. I'm going to tuck this sheet under the mattress.
4. I'm going to slip this sheet over the mattress.

Day 7 Exercise III

1. I'm pouring water into the teapot.
2. I'm pouring water into the coffee maker.
3. The water is heating up.
4. I'm pressing the switch to turn the coffee maker on.
5. The tea leaves are soaking in the hot water.

Day 8 Exercise III

1. I am pouring cereal and milk into something. It is a...
2. I am slicing a banana. I am using...
3. I am putting slices of something into the toaster. These are slices of...
4. I'm pressing the starter on the toaster. This will...
5. I'm sprinkling something on my cereal. It is...

Day 9 Exercise III

1. I'm dipping something into the yolk of an egg. What is it?
2. I'm reading something. What is it?
3. I'm wiping my lips with something. What is it?
4. I'm drinking something. What is it?
5. I'm eating something. What is it?

Day 10 Exercise III

1. I'm tying something. What am I tying?
2. I'm zipping something up. What is it?
3. I have left the house. Where am I?
4. I have put my key in something. What is it?
5. I just said, "See you later, Jenny." What was I doing?

Day 11 Exercise III

1. Oh, here's my stop.
2. M: A dollar and twenty cents, please.
   W: Okay. Here.
3. There's no room to sit down. I'll just hold on to this strap and wait.
4. I'm sitting on a bench. I wonder, will my bus be on time?

Day 12 Exercise III

1. My seat is not in the right place. It doesn't feel right.
2. (Car starting)
3. I'm driving the car.
4. I'm looking over my shoulder while I drive.
5. I'm sitting in one of the passenger seats.

Day 13 Exercise III

1. Fill it up, please.
2. M: Sixteen-fifty, ma'am.
   W: Okay. Here's seventeen.
3. I'll let this other car go first.
4. W2: The speed limit is forty-five, ma'am. You were going sixty-two.
   W1: Sorry, officer.
   W2: I'll have to write this up.
5. Unleaded, please.

Day 14 Exercise III

1. W: We're riding the train.
   M: Yes, we're both riding it.
2. I scanned my ticket, and now I'm walking through.
3. Hmm. What does this say? It says my gate is to the right.
4. Next stop is Chapman Street Station. Chapman Street Station next stop.
5. Okay. Here's my train—time for me to get on.

Day 15 Exercise III

1. Turn right at the next corner.
2. Okay. Here's eight-fifty for the fare and an extra dollar for you.
3. Taxi! Taxi!
4. I need to go to the First State Bank building.
5. You can just pull over in front of that house over there.

Day 16 Exercise III

1. I stepped over some dirt on the sidewalk.
2. I was late, so I took a shortcut.
3. I had to wait for the traffic, so I stopped at the corner.
4. I always walk in the crosswalk when I cross the street.
5. Don't run. Walk. If you're not careful, you might trip.

Day 17 Exercise III

1. I'm locking my bike to the bike rack.
2. I'm squeezing the brakes.
3. I've put on something that protects my head.
4. I'm pedaling.
5. I'm shifting gears so I can go uphill more easily.

Day 18 Exercise III

1. I'm walking up to my front door.
2. I'm taking an elevator up to where I live.
3. I'm unlocking my door, and now I'm going inside.
4. I'm taking off my work clothes and putting on some casual clothes.
5. Can you hit seven?

Day 19 Exercise III

1. I'm going to boil some water in a pan.
2. Under the pan, I lit the burner.
3. I put the basket inside the pan before the water boiled.
4. I chopped some of it up and threw the rest away.
5. Before you can steam a carrot, you have to peel it.

Day 20 Exercise III

1. I just put some spaghetti into a colander.
2. I'm stirring some spices into this sauce.
3. The sauce is boiling. I'll give it less heat.
4. Mmmm. This spaghetti is soft enough to eat now.
5. I'll just put this ground beef in here and fry it up.

Day 21 Exercise III

1. I'm measuring out two cups of rice.
2. The water is boiling.
3. The rice is ready. I just checked it.
4. I'm rinsing the rice.
5. I'm pouring off the water that has dirt and husks in it.

Day 22 Exercise III

1. I'm at the table and going to eat dinner now.
2. I'm putting something on my lap.
3. That spaghetti was good. I think I'll have some more.
4. Paul, could I have the spaghetti, please?
5. I'm putting the fork on the left side of the plate and the knife and spoon on the right.

Day 23 Exercise III

1. I put the plug in and filled the sink up.
2. I put the dishes away in the cupboard.
3. I put the dishes in the rack, and water dripped off them.
4. I put some dish soap into the water, and then I washed the dishes.
5. They were really soapy, so I rinsed them.

Day 24 Exercise III

1. When I logged on, I entered my username and password.
2. I clicked on my browser.
3. I found my friend's page at a social networking site.
4. I added a comment on her page.
5. I watched a video at a video site.

Day 25 Exercise III

1. Alex turned the volume of the music down.
2. Alex went back to the menu of his phone.
3. Alex put on his earphones.
4. Alex played a song from his playlist.
5. There were icons for many programs that would let you do specific things.

Day 26 Exercise III

1. I'm using a dictionary.
2. This caption says, "Mount Charlie, the highest point in Kent County, in the summer."
3. The title is *My Life*, and it was written by Bob Smith.
4. Hmm. What should I read? This article looks good.
5. I'm tired. I'm closing my book.

Day 27 Exercise III

1. I don't want to watch this show. It's boring.
2. I saw a commercial for a new kind of snack.
3. I picked up the remote and changed the channel.
4. During a commercial, I went to the kitchen for a snack.
5. There was nothing good on TV, so I turned it off.

Day 28 Exercise III

1. Jenny browsed through the new releases.
2. Jenny logged onto her favorite streaming service.
3. Jenny went to the living room to finish the show.
4. Jenny searched for her favorite vlogger's channel.
5. Jenny watched the livestream and chatted.

Day 29 Exercise III

1. (Yawning)
2. I turned off all the lights.
3. I changed into my nightgown.
4. I'm reading in bed.
5. Goodnight, Mom. Goodnight, Dad.

Day 30 Exercise III

1. I'm taking a basketful of laundry to the laundry room to wash.
2. I'm taking the clothes out of the washer and putting them in the dryer.
3. I'm adjusting the settings on the washer.
4. I'm putting detergent into the washer.
5. I'm folding the clothes and putting them into drawers.

Day 31 Exercise III

1. I'm emptying these wastebaskets into the garbage.
2. I'm going to recycle these cans and bottles.
3. I'm scrubbing the bathtub.
4. I'm dusting.
5. I'm bundling these up.

Day 32 Exercise III

1. My cat is purring because it's happy.
2. I'm giving the cat some fresh water.
3. I'm opening a can of food and putting it in the dish.
4. "Nice Kitty," I said, while petting my cat.
5. The cat pounced on the string while we were playing.

Day 33 Exercise III

1. I'm rinsing the car.
2. I'm buffing the car.
3. I'm vacuuming the floor.
4. I'm washing the windows of the car.
5. I'm spreading this wax on the car.

Day 34 Exercise III

1. I think you have an engine problem.
2. Is my car ready yet?
3. How much do you think it will cost?
4. Okay. I'll bring my car in so you can fix it.
5. I think it will probably cost about three hundred dollars.

Day 35 Exercise III

1. Could you give me some cheddar, please?
2. I'm getting some apples.
3. I'll have some pastrami, please.
4. I'm picking up some milk.
5. Let's see... apples, toilet paper, some pizza, milk, cheese...
6. I'll have two chicken breasts, please.

Day 36 Exercise III

1. That will be forty-six seventeen, please.
2. Can I pay by phone?
3. I'll sign there on the reader.
4. (Beeeeeep!)
5. Here's fifty.
6. Forty-six seventeen, forty-six fifty, forty-seven, forty-eight, forty-nine, and fifty.

Day 37 Exercise III

1. I'm signing my name on the back of a check.
2. Let's see. One hundred forty-eight, plus fifteen, plus thirty-two fifty gives a total of one ninety-five fifty.
3. My account number is four one nine three one seven eight.
4. Good morning. I'd like to make a deposit, please.
5. Here. I have a five-dollar bill and some change.

Day 38 Exercise III

1. To get to my email, I clicked on the browser icon.
2. I replied to a message that Tom sent me.
3. The attachment to the message was a picture.
4. This is the icon for the Internet browser.
5. I didn't want a message, so I deleted it.

Day 39 Exercise III

1. I went to the menu to find my contacts.
2. Pam selected "Text" from the menu.
3. He shined a light to find his glasses.
4. Dan used his cell phone to shine a light on a book.
5. Each number in a contacts list is called a listing.

Day 40 Exercise III

1. (Dialing a phone)
2. (Phone ringing)
3. Yes, I'm calling to see if I can get an appointment with Ms. Johnson.
4. This is Mary Taylor.
5. Hello?

Day 41 Exercise III

1. Oh, sorry.
2. Yes, could I please speak with Tom?
3. There's no one here by that name.
4. Hello?
5. W1: Well, I haven't had time for very much tennis lately.
   W2: That's too bad. Have you been working a lot?
   W1: Yeah, a lot!

Day 42 Exercise III

1. Could you please have him call me back?
2. Could I speak with Gary, please?
3. My number is five five five, seven seven two zero.
4. W: My name is Heather Gorton.
   M: Sorry. I missed that.
   W: It's Heather. Heather Gorton.
5. Chuck Harris. H-A-R-R-I-S.

Day 43

Exercise II

W: Hello?
M: Hi. Can I speak with Ted, please?
W: Uh, Ted's not available right now. Can I take a message?
M: Oh. Umm. Yeah, could you please? My name is Bob. I'm on Ted's basketball team.
W: Hi, Bob. I'm Ted's sister, Karen.
M: Hi, Karen. Anyway, could you tell Ted that our game tonight is canceled?
W: Sure. I'm writing it down on some notepaper now. Game canceled.
M: Thanks. I hope he gets it in time.
W: I'm sure he will. I'm putting the message right next to the phone.
M: Thanks.

Exercise III

1. Hello?
2. Please tell him that Greg called.
3. Would you like me to take a message?
4. Greg. This is Jason. I'm just calling you back.
5. Is Jason there, please?

Day 44 Exercise III

1. I'm testing my webcam to make sure it works.
2. I'm inviting people to a video call.
3. Tom is sharing his screen with us.
4. We're discussing our homework together.
5. Pam is not answering the invite I sent.

Day 45 Exercise III

1. I'm posting this photo online.
2. I'm writing a comment on my friend's post.
3. I'm adding some effects to this photo.
4. Jenny is checking her feed.
5. Jenny's friends are leaving comments on her post.

Day 46 Exercise III

1. M2: Regular mail or express?
   M1: Regular, please.
2. I'm waiting in line at the post office.
3. M2: Regular mail or express?
   M1: Express mail, please.
4. W: Can you give me postage for this letter?
   M: That'll be a dollar twenty, please.
5. I'm putting a letter on the scale.

Day 47 Exercise III

1. I'm going to Leo's birthday party.
2. Could I have some more ice cream and birthday cake?
3. This is a great present. Thank you.
4. Come on. Time for everyone to sing.
5. I'm signing a card and wrapping a present for the party.

Day 48 Exercise III

1. Could I have two large popcorns, please?
2. Coming soon to a theater near you...
3. Here's your stub back, sir. Enjoy the show.
4. M: Could I have two tickets for *Into the Clouds*, please?
   W: Sixteen fifty, please.
5. Let's see, there's a show at four fifteen, and then another at seven forty.

Day 49 Exercise III

1. I'd like one small cola, please.
2. M: That will be four twenty-five.
   M: Okay. Here's a five.
3. I'm eating my food in the restaurant.
4. I'm taking my food outside the restaurant.
5. I'm putting these empty wrappers in the trash.

Day 50 Exercise III

1. Do you want your coffee for here or to go?
2. The Wi-Fi at the shop was free.
3. The clerk was standing at the counter.
4. She finished her coffee and got a refill.
5. They put their cups on a tray for dirty dishes.

Answer Key

Day 1 First Thing in the Morning

I. 1. waking up 2. shaving
3. washing 4. ringing
5. drying off 6. brushing hair

II. a. 2, 1 b. 1, 2 c. 2, 1
d. 1, 2 e. 1, 2

III. 1. waking up 2. taking a shower
3. shaving 4. eating breakfast

Day 2 Brushing Your Teeth / Flossing

I. 1. up and down 2. running
3. rinsing 4. spitting
5. back and forth 6. squeezing

II. 1. e 2. b 3. c
4. a 5. d

III. 1. between his teeth 2. in a rack
3. his mouth 4. a tube

Day 3 Taking a Shower

I. 1. stepping out 2. drying off
3. turning on 4. turning off
5. pulling shut 6. wrapping

II. 1. b 2. e 3. d
4. a 5. c

III. 1. soap 2. a towel
3. a blow dryer 4. deodorant

Day 4 Getting Dressed: A Man

I. 1. buckling 2. buttoning
3. zipping up 4. tucking
5. pulling 6. straightening

II. *some:* glasses, pants, shoes, socks, underwear
a: jacket, shirt

III. a. 2 b. 7 c. 4
d. 9 e. 1 f. 6
g. 8 h. 3 i. 5

Day 5 Getting Dressed: A Woman

I. 1. putting on 2. inside
3. outside 4. wearing
5. going 6. wrapping

II. 1. b 2. e 3. a
4. c 5. d

III. a. 4 b. 3 c. 5
d. 6 e. 1 f. 2

Day 6 Making a Bed

I. 1. fluffing up 2. spreading
3. smoothing out 4. slipping
5. tucking 6. pulling

II. a. 5 b. 1 c. 4
d. 2 e. 3 f. 6

III. 1. bedspread 2. pillowcase
3. tuck 4. slip

Day 7 Making Coffee / Making Tea

I. 1. heating 2. pouring
3. dripping 4. scooping
5. turning 6. straining

II. 1. e 2. a 3. b
4. d 5. c

III. 1. teapot 2. pouring
3. heating 4. switch
5. hot

Day 8 Preparing Breakfast

I. 1. popping 2. sprinkling
3. peeling 4. cracking
5. spreading 6. slicing

II. 1. bowl 2. knife
3. a slice of bread 4. butter
5. cereal box 6. jam

III. 1. bowl 2. a knife
3. bread 4. lower the bread
5. sugar

Day 9 Eating Breakfast

I. 1. reading 2. dipping
3. drinking 4. sitting
5. wiping 6. leaving

II. 1. spoon 2. fork
3. toast 4. knife
5. bowl 6. egg
7. bacon

III. 1. toast 2. the news
3. a napkin 4. coffee
5. breakfast

Day 10 Leaving the House

I. 1. putting on 2. shutting
3. picking up 4. putting
5. opening 6. zipping up

II. 1. b 2. e
3. c 4. d
5. a

III. 1. shoes 2. a jacket
3. outside 4. a pocket
5. saying goodbye

Day 11 Taking a Bus

I. 1. pressing 2. due
3. full 4. paying
5. walking 6. waiting

II. 1. a 2. e 3. d
4. b 5. c

III. 1. ringing a signal 2. paying a bus driver
3. standing 4. waiting for a bus

Day 12 Starting a Car

I. 1. pressing 2. looking
3. backing 4. adjusting
5. shifting 6. buckling

II. 1. c 2. e
3. d 4. a
5. b

III. a. 2 b. 3
c. 4 d. 5
e. 1

Day 13 Driving Along

I. 1. turning right 2. turning left
3. getting off 4. changing lanes
5. going straight 6. getting on

II. 1. e 2. a 3. d
4. c 5. b

III. a. 4 b. 1 c. 2
d. 5 e. 3

Day 14 Taking a Train

I. 1. getting on 2. buying
3. standing 4. getting off
5. scanning 6. waiting

II. 1. d 2. a 3. b
4. c 5. e

III. 1. passengers 2. gate
3. sign 4. announced
5. arrived

Day 15 Taking a Taxi

I. 1. giving 2. checking
3. starting 4. paying
5. hailing 6. getting into

II. 1. d 2. c 3. e
4. b 5. a

III. a. 3 b. 2 c. 1
d. 5 e. 4

Day 16 Walking Somewhere

I. 1. crossing 2. stepping
3. taking 4. running
5. tripping 6. stopping

II. 1. a 2. d 3. c
4. b 5. e

III. 1. stepped 2. late
3. traffic 4. crosswalk
5. trip

Day 17 Riding a Bicycle

I. 1. squeezing 2. pedaling
3. holding 4. swinging
5. locking 6. shifting

II. 1. pedals 2. gears
3. helmet 4. handlebars
5. brakes 6. shift lever

III. a. 2 b. 1 c. 4
d. 5 e. 3

Day 18 Returning Home

I. 1. walking 2. getting
3. taking 4. setting
5. hanging 6. pressing

II. 1. d 2. b 3. c
4. e 5. a

III. a. 4 b. 5 c. 2
d. 3 e. 1

Day 19 Preparing Vegetables

I. 1. slicing 2. peeling
3. throwing 4. mixing
5. boiling 6. steaming

II. 1. a 2. e
3. d 4. b
5. c

III. 1. water 2. lit
3. inside 4. chopped
5. carrot

Day 20 Making Spaghetti

I. 1. pouring 2. boiling
3. ladling 4. dicing
5. frying 6. stirring

II. 1. a 2. e 3. c
4. b 5. d

III. 1. draining 2. adding
3. down 4. tender
5. frying pan

Day 21 Cooking Rice

I. 1. spooning 2. measuring
3. rinsing 4. getting rid of
5. boiling 6. pouring

II. 1. b 2. c 3. a
4. d 5. e

III. a. 1 b. 5 c. 4
d. 3 e. 2

Day 22 Eating Dinner

I. 1. setting 2. sitting
3. putting 4. helping
5. having 6. passing

II. 1. salad bowl 2. coffee cup
3. fork 4. napkin
5. glass 6. plate
7. spoon 8. knife

III. 1. sitting 2. napkin
3. a second helping 4. pass something
5. setting the table

Day 23 Cleaning Up

I. 1. offering 2. scraping
3. carrying 4. stacking
5. throwing 6. wiping

II. 1. a 2. e 3. b
4. d 5. c

III. 1. put the plug 2. cupboard
3. water dripped 4. washed
5. rinsed

Day 24 Using the Internet

I. 1. turned 2. typed
3. clicked 4. went
5. read 6. added

II. 1. d 2. c 3. a
4. e 5. b

III. 1. logged on 2. clicked
3. social networking 4. added
5. site

Day 25 Listening to Music

I. 1. connected 2. adjusted
3. tapped 4. looked through
5. selected 6. held

II. 1. d 2. a
3. e 4. b
5. c

III. 1. softer 2. swiped
3. connected 4. tapped
5. apps

Day 26 Reading

I. 1. closing 2. turning 3. reading 4. looking up 5. looking at 6. opening
II. 1. table of contents 2. title 3. author's name 4. cover 5. caption 6. page number
III. 1. looking up 2. next to a picture 3. cover 4. found 5. finished

Day 27 Watching Television

I. 1. turning up 2. ending 3. watching 4. turning on 5. turning off 6. changing
II. 1. b 2. e 3. c 4. a 5. d
III. 1. show 2. commercial 3. remote 4. went 5. turned it off

Day 28 Streaming Services

I. 1. browsed 2. subscribed 3. changed 4. searched 5. watched 6. went
II. 1. e 2. b 3. d 4. c 5 a
III. 1. browsed 2. streaming 3. finish 4. searched 5. livestream

Day 29 Going to Bed

I. 1. lying 2. going 3. setting 4. getting 5. hanging 6. yawning
II. 1. e 2. b 3. c 4. a 5. d
III. a. 1 b. 5 c. 2 d. 4 e. 3

Day 30 Doing Laundry

I. 1. spinning 2. drying 3. washing 4. checking 5. sorting 6. folding
II. 1. e 2. c 3. d 4. a 5. b
III. a. 3 b. 4 c. 2 d. 5 e. 1

Day 31 Cleaning the House

I. 1. sweeping 2. mopping 3. throwing 4. wiping 5. scrubbing 6. vacuuming
II. 1. broom 2. dustpan 3. bucket 4. wastebasket 5. garbage bag 6. garbage can
III. 1. throwing 2. recycling 3. bathroom 4. furniture 5. newspapers

Day 32 Taking Care of Pets

I. 1. playing 2. feeding 3. petting 4. putting 5. cleaning 6. purring
II. 1. c 2. d 3. a 4. e 5. b
III. 1. purring 2. fresh 3. can 4. petting 5. pounced

Day 33 Cleaning a Car

I. 1. wiping 2. spreading 3. rinsing 4. washing 5. drying 6. dipping
II. 1. e 2. c 3. a 4. b 5. d
III. a. 2 b. 3 c. 1 d. 5 e. 4

Day 34 Taking a Car to a Garage for Repairs

I. 1. taking 2. working 3. asking 4. giving 5. calling 6. coming
II. 1. b 2. e 3. a 4. c 5. d
III. 1. diagnosing 2. pick up 3. an estimate 4. get her car fixed 5. estimating

Day 35 Shopping for Groceries

I. 1. weighing 2. trying 3. putting 4. taking 5. going 6. choosing
II. 1. a 2. c 3. b 4. d 5. e
III. a. 5 b. 1 c. 3 d. 6 e. 4 f. 2

Day 36 Paying for Things

I. 1. counting 2. scanning 3. unlocking 4. pressing 5. signing 6. inserting
II. 1. c 2. d 3. b 4. a 5. e
III. a. 2 b. 5 c. 6 d. 4 e. 1 f. 3

Day 37 Going to a Bank

I. 1. filling out 2. checking 3. printing 4. going 5. endorsing 6. giving
II. 1. b 2. c 3. d 4. e 5. a
III. 1. endorsing 2. total 3. account number 4. window 5. some cash

Day 38 Getting and Sending Email

I. 1. clicked 2. log in 3. opened 4. replied to 5. printed 6. deleted
II. 1. a 2. c 3. d 4. e 5. b
III. 1. clicked 2. replied 3. attachment 4. icon 5. deleted

Day 39 Using a Mobile Phone / Texting

I. 1. dialed 2. pick up
3. answered 4. texted
5. shined 6. took

II. 1. b 2. e 3. d
4. a 5. c

III. 1. went 2. selected "Text"
3. shined 4. shine
5. listing

Day 40 Making a Phone Call

I. 1. identifying 2. unlocking
3. looking up 4. dialing
5. picking up 6. answering

II. 1. e 2. a 3. d
4. b 5. c

III. a. 2 b. 5 c. 3
d. 4 e. 1

Day 41 Answering a Telephone

I. 1. telling 2. answering
3. talking 4. hanging up
5. taking 6. apologizing

II. 1. d 2. b 3. e
4. a 5. c

III. a. 4 b. 5 c. 2
d. 3 e. 1

Day 42 Leaving a Message

I. 1. agreeing 2. spelling
3. repeating 4. leaving
5. identifying 6. asking

II. 1. c 2. a 3. b
4. e 5. d

III. a. 2 b. 1 c. 4
d. 5 e. 3

Day 43 Taking a Message

I. 1. writing 2. offering
3. asking 4. returning
5. leaving 6. answering

II. 1. with 2. for
3. on 4. next to
5. about

III. a. 1 b. 5 c. 4
d. 2 e. 3

Day 44 Video Conferencing

I. 1. turning on 2. sharing
3. testing 4. selecting
5. discussing 6. answered

II. 1. c 2. a 3. e
4. b 5. d

III. 1. testing 2. inviting
3. sharing 4. discussing
5. answering

Day 45 Posting on Social Media

I. 1. opening 2. adding
3. writing 4. commenting
5. uploading 6. looking

II. 1. a 2. d
3. c 4. b
5. e

III. 1. posting 2. writing
3. adding 4. checking
5. leaving

Day 46 Mailing a Letter

I. 1. folding 2. enclosing
3. sealing 4. licking
5. writing 6. sticking

II. 1. b 2. e 3. a
4. c 5. d

III. a. 5 b. 3 c. 2
d. 4 e. 1

Day 47 Going to a Party

I. 1. giving 2. singing
3. wrapping 4. blowing
5. lighting 6. signing

II. 1. a 2. d 3. c
4. b 5. e

III. 1. going 2. ice cream
3. present 4. sing
5. wrapping

Day 48 Going to a Movie

I. 1. buying 2. watching
3. tearing 4. giving
5. going 6. finding

II. 1. e 2. a 3. b
4. c 5. d

III. 1. popcorn 2. a preview
3. tore 4. box office
5. when the movie is showing

Day 49 Eating at a Fast-Food Restaurant

I. 1. standing 2. reading
3. eating 4. paying
5. ordering 6. throwing

II. 1. a 2. b 3. d
4. c 5. e

III. a. 5 b. 3 c. 4
d. 1 e. 2

Day 50 Having Coffee at a Coffee Shop

I. 1. ordered 2. drink
3. punched 4. pumped
5. sat down 6. plugged

II. 1. c 2. e 3. a
4. d 5. b

III. 1. for here 2. was free
3. counter 4. finished
5. dirty

Memo